SEARCH FOR A METHOD

SEARCH
FOR A METHOD

JEAN-PAUL SARTRE

Translated from the French and with an Introduction by

HAZEL E. BARNES

VINTAGE BOOKS

A Division of Random House

New York

AU CASTOR

◌◌◌◌◌◌◌◌◌◌◌◌◌◌◌◌◌◌◌◌◌◌◌◌◌◌◌

INTRODUCTION

W HAT we call freedom is the irreducibility of the cultural order to the natural order." In the early sixties Sartre is as far removed as ever from any view that would reduce man to his biology, or history to the mechanistic functioning of immanent laws, natural or economic. But what of the individual's relation to his culture?

In *Being and Nothingness,* published in 1943, the answer was clear. Sartre was recognized as the proponent of the most radical view of human freedom to appear since the Epicureans. Hostile critics, from both the Left and the Right, attacked him for giving too little emphasis to hereditary and environmental conditioning. They said that his philosophy allowed no room for any positive social theory. The individual consciousness was splendidly independent—and alone.

In 1960 Sartre proved the critics wrong. His *Critique of Dialectical Reason* presented a carefully worked out social and political philosophy which analyzed the relation of the human being to the physical universe, to the group, to the nation, to history—providing, in short, a total view of man's position in-the-world. At the same time it brought into focus a new and important question which has been asked with increasing urgency during the past few years. Sartre has aligned himself more and more closely with Marxism. It has been generally assumed that Marxism and existentialism are irreconcilable. Had Sartre then betrayed one for the other? In the *Critique* Sartre does not hedge. The only philosophy today, he says, is Marxism. Existentialism is but a subordinate ideology which, working from within, attempts to influence the future development of Marxism. "It is a parasitical system living on the margin of Knowledge, which at first it opposed but into which today it seeks to be integrated." [1]

This startling statement immediately forces us to ask ourselves how we are to place this new work. Who is this Sartre? What are we to make of him? Consistency in detail is not important; if we want a philosopher to develop throughout his lifetime, the last thing to demand of him is that he fit his new thought to the measure of his own printed word. But when what is involved is the over-all view and the fundamental principles that support it, then we want to know where we stand. Contemporary Marxists generally hold that we are culturally and economically conditioned; they leave no place for freedom. If Sartre's declaration for Marxism means that in his opinion men are not free after all, then those of us who have found his existentialism a significant philosophy in the past will respect Sartre's decision, but we will regretfully decline to follow him. We, for our part, will not give the name of existentialism to determinism, whatever Sartre may wish to do. But perhaps the opposite is true. If Sartre has found a way of reconciling existentialism with Marxism, if what he does is not to forget the free individual of existentialism but rather to make room for him in a Marxist framework, then the

[1] *Search for a Method*, p. 8.

situation is totally different. We may quibble as to whether we wish to call this new philosophy neo-Marxism or neo-existentialism. There will be some who will still prefer the early Sartre to the later one. But we will have to grant that Sartre has fulfilled his promise—to show how the free individual described in *Being and Nothingness* may commit himself meaningfully in the world.

Search for a Method (*Question de Méthode* is the French title) is a separate essay published together with a much longer treatise, *Critique of Dialectical Reason,* which gives its title to the total work.[2] Sartre says that *Search for a Method* logically belongs at the end of the *Critique,* since it is the *Critique* which supplies the critical foundations for the method which Sartre proposes. He places the shorter essay first, partly because he feared it might otherwise seem that "the mountain had brought forth a mouse" and partly because *Search for a Method* was actually written first. I think it doubtful whether anyone but its author would feel that its present position is illogical. It is the search for a method by which the existentialist Marxist may hope to understand both individual persons and history. It sets forth specifically those ways in which existentialism seeks to modify Marxism and to change its direction. It outlines its proposed progressive-regressive method and defines its own relation to other intellectual disciplines. In accomplishing this, Sartre clarifies his own

[2] To be precise, the title page reads: *Critique de la raison dialectique* (*précédé de Question de méthode*). In his preface to the volume as a whole, Sartre uses the plural *Questions* when referring to the first essay. In my Introduction, quotations from *Search for a Method* are identified by reference to appropriate pages in this translation. When quoting from the second, as yet untranslated, essay, I refer simply to the *Critique;* page numbers are based on the French edition published by Gallimard in 1960.

view of the nature of history and the individual's relation to history. *Search for a Method* is complete in itself. Yet Sartre is right in saying that its true significance must be appreciated against the background of the rest of the work. Only the first volume of *Critique of Dialectical Reason* has as yet been published. It consists of 755 pages of small type, about a hundred of which go to make up *Search for a Method*. The rest of the book discusses the nature of dialectical reason, the material aspect of human existence, the movement from individual action to group activity and from the group to history.

The title, *Critique of Dialectical Reason*, suggests both Kant and Hegel. Like Kant in *Critique of Pure Reason*, Sartre is concerned with the nature, possibilities, and limitations of human reason. But there the resemblance ends, for Sartre's interest is not primarily epistemological or even metaphysical. The greater debt is to Hegel, and Sartre acknowledges it in his preface. Through Marxism, he says, existentialism has inherited and retains two things from Hegel: First, the view that if there is to be any Truth in man's understanding of himself, it must be a Truth which *becomes;* Truth is something which emerges. And second, what Truth must become is a totalization. "In *Search for a Method*," Sartre says, "I have taken it for granted that such a totalization is perpetually in process as History and as historical Truth." Sartre continues to believe, as Hegel did, that the events of history may be interpreted as a dialectical process wherein existing contradictions give rise to a new synthesis which surpasses them. He rejects completely, of course, Hegel's concept of Absolute Mind making itself concrete through the dialectic. Nevertheless, he states—and this, I think, one would not have anticipated from *Being and Nothingness*—that the synthetic surpassing loses all meaning if, as the positivists claim, there are only multiple histories and truths. In searching for a History and a Truth that are totalizing, Sartre asks whether there is not *a* Truth of man, whether we may speak of a single History of man. The problem of History as such is reserved for the second volume of the *Critique,* which, we are told, will deal with "History in process and Truth in its becoming." That there is a Truth of man Sartre makes plain in his first essay. It is not true that man is unknowable, but only that he is still unknown and that we have not yet had at our disposal the proper instruments for learning to know him. To understand man, we must develop a "philosophical anthropology." The existing tools and methods of the natural sciences, of traditional sociology and anthropology, are not adequate. What is needed is a new kind of Reason.

Sartre points out that nobody, not even the most radical empiricist, is willing to limit Reason to the mere order of our thoughts. According to the philosophy which one holds, one may claim that Reason reproduces the order of Being or that it imposes an order on Being. But Reason is in any case a relation between Being and knowing. Thus Sartre maintains that the relation between the historical totalization and the totalizing Truth is a moving relationship involving both Being and knowing. As such it is properly called a Reason. But this new dialectical relation between thought and its object demands a new kind of Reason. In short, we are offered a "dialectical reason." (It is important to remember that "dialectic" refers both to the connection between objective events and to the method of knowing and fixing these events.)

Since Marx, the concept of dialectic has always been

linked with materialism. Perhaps the best way to approach Sartre's "dialectical reason" is to consider what he has to say about matter.

In *Being and Nothingness* the central issue was the distinction between Being-in-itself, or non-conscious reality, and Being-for-itself, the Being of the human person. Consciousness brought significance and meaning to the world by effecting a psychic cleavage, or nothingness, between itself and the objects of which it was conscious. Without this "shell of nothingness," Being remained an undifferentiated plenitude. About Being-in-itself one could say only that "Being is." Thus the world of matter or of nature was an irrational world where form and unity and multiplicity emerged only through the activity of a consciousness. As man encounters this world, he views it as a field of instrumental possibilities. He uses it for his projects, relating himself to it through his body. But the material is not limitlessly malleable. Like the painter's pigments, it represents both possibilities for use and what Sartre, following Bachelard, calls a "coefficient of resistance."

This position is all very well for a philosophy of consciousness or for a phenomenology. But how does it relate to a doctrine of dialectical materialism? Sartre begins with a statement that suggests a considerable modification of his earlier view.

> Ought we then to deny the existence of dialectical connections at the center of inanimate Nature? Not at all. To tell the truth, I do not see that we are, at the present stage of our knowledge, in a position either to affirm or to deny. Each one is free to *believe* that physico-chemical laws express a dialectical reason or *not to believe* it.[3]

[3] *Critique*, p. 129.

Sartre goes on to say that the possibility that we may someday discover the existence of a "concrete dialectic of Nature" must be kept open. As for man, he is one material being among others and enjoys no privileged status. Yet Sartre rejects the view that human events are determined by any sort of external law imposed upon them. Today's Marxists, he says, have indeed tried to maintain a "dialectic without men," and this is precisely what has caused Marxism to stagnate and turned it into "a paranoiac dream."

Even granting that a dialectic of nature just might exist, there are two reasons why we cannot make it a support for dialectical materialism as it is usually conceived. In the first place, it could at present be only "a metaphysical hypothesis." To treat it as an unconditioned law driving men to make History by blind necessity, is to substitute "obscurity for clarity, conjecture for evidence, science fiction for Truth." There is another, stronger reason. Even though neither God nor Nature has allotted to man a privileged position, there still remains in his consciousness that power of effecting a nothingness, or putting a psychic distance between itself and its objects. Hence man is never one with the matter around him. Sartre points out that matter as such—that is, as Being which is totally devoid of any human signification—is never encountered in human experience. "Matter could be matter only for God or for pure matter, which would be absurd." [4] The world which man knows and lives in is a human world. Even if it could be shown that there are dialectical connections in Nature, man would still have to take them to his own account, to establish his own relations with them. The only dialectical materialism which makes

[4] *Critique,* p. 247.

sense is a "historical materialism," a materialism viewed from inside the history of man's relation with matter.

The human project remains central in Sartre's thought. Man makes his being by launching himself toward the future. He can do so only by inscribing himself in the world of matter.

> At each instant we experience material reality as a threat against our life, as a resistance to our work, as a limit to our knowing, and as an instrumentality already revealed or possible.[5]

Man's way of being is his way of relating himself to the world. There could be no relation without the free consciousness which allows man to assume a point of view on the world. But man would be equally unable to have any connection with matter if he did not himself possess a materiality. In this way Sartre arrives at a definition of work, one which could just as well be applied to any human activity.

> The meaning of human work is the fact that man reduces himself to inorganic materiality in order to act materially upon matter and to change his material life. By transubstantiation, the project, which, by means of our body, is inscribed in the thing, takes on the substantial characteristics of that thing without entirely losing its own original qualities.[6]

In any human activity in the world there is an interchange. The person cloaks the thing with a human signification, but in return, his action, by becoming objectified in the realm of matter, is at least in part reified, made into a thing. Sartre says that men are things to the exact degree that things are human. It is only through

[5] Ibid.
[6] Ibid., p. 246.

this "transubstantiation" that we can speak of a future for either man or things.

Objectively and abstractly this view of the relation between men and things does not appear essentially different from Sartre's earlier position. But Sartre makes one change which puts all the existential structures in a new light. In *Being and Nothingness,* consciousness, which *is* freedom, recognizes itself in anguish. Perhaps even more basically, it experiences itself as desire. In the *Critique* Sartre says that the fundamental existential structure of man is *need* (*besoin*). The substitution may appear trivial; actually its consequences are all-pervasive. *Desire* suggests the possibility of unrestricted movement, of a freedom which may change the objects of its desire at will. *Need* brings in something from the outside, a necessity which man cannot ultimately escape, no matter how much he may vary his reaction to it. And *need,* Sartre tells us, is itself related to *scarcity.* There is simply *not enough* of the kinds of matter to which *need* directs its demands.

Man's inhumanity to man is not, for Sartre, a fact of human nature. There is no human nature if by this we mean an innate disposition to adopt certain attitudes and conduct rather than others. But against the background of need and scarcity man—every man—assumes for himself and for others a dimension which is non-human. The fact of scarcity forces upon humanity the realization that it is impossible for *all* human beings to coexist. Every man is potentially a bringer of death to each other man. Sartre says:

Nothing—neither wild beasts nor microbes—can be more terrible for man than a cruel, intelligent, flesh-eating species which could understand and thwart human intelligence and whose aim would be precisely

the destruction of man. This species is obviously our
own . . . in a milieu of scarcity.[7]

When he speaks of scarcity, Sartre means both the lack
of the most immediate things which enable men to stay
alive and the lack of those other things which are necessary to make people's lives satisfying, once they have got
beyond the problem of mere subsistence. Society
"chooses its expendables." Through the established social structure, it determines whether to combat scarcity
by means of birth control or by letting natural forces
handle the problem of overpopulation. It decides
whether the hazards of existence will be shared equally
by all of its members, or whether it will organize itself
into sharply divided classes, each living at the expense
of the other. In certain colonial societies, Sartre claims,
the colonialists deliberately designate "the natives" as
sub-men, keeping for themselves the appellation of the
truly human. Or in extreme cases the masses of men support a small minority who live among them as gods.
The material fact of scarcity is there at the start, but human action makes out of the material fact a specific social pattern.

From one point of view, history might be said to be
the story of how human *praxis* has inscribed itself in
the *pratico-inerte*. The two terms *praxis* and *pratico-
inerte* are not to be equated with "Being-for-itself" and
"Being-in-itself," but there is a sense in which they hold
equivalent positions in Sartre's most recent work. *Praxis*
(the Greek word for "action") is any meaningful or purposeful human activity, any act which is not mere random, undirected motion. The *pratico-inerte* is more
than just matter, though it certainly includes the material environment. It comprises all those things which go

[7] Ibid., p. 208.

to make up man's experience of finitude. In his play *No Exit* Sartre declared that Hell is other people. Now he says that Hell is the *pratico-inerte*, for it "steals my action from me." By simply being there—or even by not being there—matter provokes certain actions and prevents others. Granted that man as a material being needs warmth, the presence or absence of coal in a country conditions the lives of the inhabitants. More than this, the "active inertia" of the *pratico-inerte* can distort and change the ends I work toward. It can impose upon my actions a "counter-finality." For example, a community may clear the timber from a hillside in order to have more cultivable land, but this end may be submerged and overwhelmed in the floods and erosion resulting from the absence of trees. The counter-finality is the end result of the human action, and at the same time it is opposed to the end which the agents had intended. One finds one's *praxis* deviated by the sheer weight of space and time. Concerted group action may be prevented by the mere distance between its members. The continuity of a historical movement is broken or distorted by the "rupture between the generations." Yet while we must acknowledge the weight of external factors in determining the ultimate outcome of human endeavor, we recognize that *praxis* is at the start and at the finish.

It is possible to see history as nothing more than the record of a plurality of individuals inscribing their *praxis* upon the passive unity of the *pratico-inerte* in a milieu of scarcity. But this is not to take the point of view of dialectic. Sartre defines man as the being who possesses the *possibility of making history*. The realization of this possibility emerges with the dialectical process. Sartre says that primitive "societies of repetition" are pre-historic or non-historic. This is because they have met the problem of scarcity in such a way that they have established an exact equilibrium, one which causes them to live life as if in ritualistic myth. History begins only when some unexpected event effects a rupture, thus bringing into being a contradiction. In the attempt to surpass the contradiction, men create a new synthesis, which changes their world; and history is born. Men can make history without being aware of the history they are making. There are many different ways in which they may look backward and try to interpret past events. But Marxism alone, says Sartre, offers an interpretation which is valid. Moreover, Marxism is "history itself become conscious of itself"; Marxism lives its present history with full awareness that it is outlining the history of the future.

Two questions immediately arise. In what sense does Sartre mean that Marxism is the only valid interpretation? And does this mean that History is an external force imposed upon men, forcing them to follow certain patterns willy-nilly? To take up the second question first, the answer is clear. Sartre admits that most contemporary Marxists write as if History were an immanent force and men mere counters shoved along by it, but he says this to reproach them. Marx himself, Sartre points out, never held this view, and even Engels did not wholly embrace it. Both Marx and Engels stated their position in a sentence which Sartre accepts completely: "Men make their history upon the basis of prior conditions." Most Marxists have chosen to interpret the statement as if it said merely that men are conditioned. Sartre never denies the existence of the conditions, but he insists (as Marx did) that it is still men who *make* the history. This is because the most fundamental characteristic of man as consciousness is his ability to go beyond his situation. He is never identical with it, but rather exists as a relation to it. Thus he determines how he will live it and what its meaning is to be; he is not determined by it. At the same time he cannot exist except in a situation, and the process by which he goes beyond or surpasses it must in some way include the particular conditions which go to make up the situation. Men make history by this continual surpassing. There is no immanent law, no hyperorganism hovering above men's relations with one another, no set mechanism gradually releasing its pre-established effects. Human events do not happen as the result of any external schema of causation, nor should they ever be fitted into any a priori schema of interpretation.

Then how can they be said to fit into the philosophy of dialectical materialism? Sartre presupposes a background of Marxism rather than restating explicitly the fundamental principles of Marx which he embraces. Nevertheless, we can readily detect the broad Marxist concepts which he has adopted. There is first of all the idea that the mode of men's lives in past and present societies is directly determined by the mode and the relations of production and the socio-economic structures which have been built upon them. Man is the product of his own product, though Sartre hastens to add that he is also a historical agent, who can never be made only a product. Second, since man's attempt to solve the problems of production has taken the form of building up a class society, we must interpret history as being in large part the history of the class struggle. Man will not have true political freedom so long as class distinctions remain. Third, the dominant ideas and values of a period are the ideas and values of the dominant class. The individual expresses his class in his creative work as in his everyday behavior. Finally, there is no truth in the old idea that history is a forward march, a progress toward some distant perfection. But at the same time history displays a certain inevitability in its broad outlines, and it is here that we see the traces of a dialectical movement. Dialectic is not a determinism—at least not for Sartre. Men submit to dialectic just insofar as they make history dialectically. The existence of class structure in the milieu of scarcity gives rise to certain contradictions. Attempts at a healing synthesis create in turn new contradictions, and the process cannot be finally resolved until the coming into being of a classless society and the final solving of the problems of production. For the class structure is itself a contradiction. As Sartre points out, those who do the work of production do not own the instruments of production. In societies where there is economic oppression, the employer tries to make use of the distinctively human qualities of the worker while making him a thing, treating him as an object. The ultimate alienation of man today is found in the interchangeability of the men who run the machines.[8]

We may find a connecting link between the philoso-

---

[8] I do not think that this Introduction is an appropriate place for me to discuss the history of the gradual development of Sartre's thought in connection with Marxism and Communism. *Search for a Method* is a theoretical treatise, not an analysis of specific political issues. I will state here merely that Sartre does not identify Marxism and Communism and that he has never done so. Nor does he believe that the "dictatorship of the Proletariat" ever actually existed in the Soviet Union or elsewhere; in fact he calls the concept a contradiction in terms (*Critique*, pp. 629–30). *Search for a Method* makes clear that the Marxism which he embraces is closely allied to the work of Marx himself and far removed from what recent writers have made of Marx. The most important fact is that Sartre believes Marxism has only begun to develop, even on its theoretical side.

pher of the free consciousness and the Marxist theoretician if we recall that whenever Sartre has written about freedom, the concept has always had a double aspect. Freedom is a fact, and it is the object of an imperative. To say that man is free is to say that he is reponsible for what he does; it is also to say that he has the possibility of living creatively. But a society which through economic oppression or terror does everything to thwart the individual's creative act, which turns constructive ends into disastrous counter-finalities, leaves man his freedom only as a sort of abstraction. Psychological freedom and political freedom are inextricable even though they are not identical: first, because man cannot fight for his political freedom unless he is free and can recognize that he is so; second, because any society which seeks to justify oppression must base itself upon the false premise that men are not free beings who make themselves what they are, but that they are born with an absolute nature bound up with some accident of birth. Thus it is because men are existentially free that Sartre demands for them a political and practical freedom.

This double aspect continues in the *Critique*. Man lives by "internalizing the external." By his free act of consciousness, he takes what is outside and makes of it a structure of his inner life. But no matter what attitude he may take toward the environment—whether unthinking acceptance or rebellion—he must objectify himself through his acts in the *pratico-inerte*. The result is that for the most part he freely realizes himself as being what he already is. A woman working in a factory for subsistence wages may decide after careful calculation that the role of mother is closed to her; her situation, says Sartre, has already determined what she takes to her own account. The man who must spend all his wages in order to keep himself alive does not objectify himself in the same world of merchandise as the man whose salary opens a wide range of choices. When choosing a career the young man from a bourgeois family sees the world offering a variety of pathways to a professional life; the boy in a worker's family sees most of these paths already barred off.

Sartre never denies that the individual determines the peculiar quality of the life chosen within these conditions. Every life is unique. When he wrote *Being and Nothingness*, he was apparently satisfied to let it go at that. The Marxist Sartre adds two things which do not alter the original position but considerably change the way we look at it. First, he says that the individual's act expresses not only the person who performs it but also the class to which the person belongs. He gives as an example the colored member of an air-force ground crew whose country's laws forbid him ever to become a pilot. If the man secretly steals a plane and flies it, his act is a rebellion, a refusal to accept the condition which society has imposed upon him. It is a choice of death or imprisonment over the degradation of his situation. But it is at the same time an expression of his class and the present state of its self-conscious movement toward liberation. The pilot indicates more than himself by his act. He points to a particular stage at which his class has initiated the moment of refusal but not yet found adequate instruments for collective action. There is more involved here than the question of interpretation. For Sartre, the reality of class carries as much weight as the purely material structures in the *pratico-inerte*. They are part of that external which must be internalized, and there must occur here that same "transubstantiation" which we observed in the relation between persons and things. The class structure and the characteristics of a particular class depend upon the addition of each individual *praxis,* but each *praxis* is conditioned and deviated in the milieu of the already existing class. Sartre goes to great pains to show how everyone from childhood on inscribes his own history by means of the instruments and against the obstacles offered by his social environment. I come into being in a community to which my parents have already sworn my commitments. I am born under a vow (*assermenté*). The language which I speak, the common ideas which I meet and use in formulating my attitudes—all these "steal my thought from me," either by conditioning it at the start or by twisting it, putting upon it a counter-finality after I have formulated it, so that its end-expression is taken as something other than I intended. It is in this way that man finds himself to be "the product of his own product."

Technically Sartre prepared us for this view in *Being and Nothingness.* There he allowed two limits to freedom: (1) The fact that I exist at all and my existing as a free being do not depend on me. I am not free not to be free. Necessity compels me to exert my free act of choice in "internalizing the external." (2) My freedom is limited by the freedom of the other person. It is the second of these limitations to which Sartre has given a new emphasis. He continues to insist that only human beings can make an object of man. But he goes much further in the direction of seeing man as really made an object. He attaches more significance to the conditioning of the inward life—though he never quite wipes out the tiny *décalage,* the gap or nothingness which lies between the individual and the situation in which he finds himself. What is more important is the fact that now his interest lies much more with the degree of practical freedom people experience than with the psychological freedom which most ignore or seek to evade. Many of Sartre's critics in the forties were willing to agree with him that man is free in the sense that at any moment there is always more than one choice theoretically open to him. Man can usually choose either to submit or to die; if he is about to die, he can choose how he will meet his death. But they felt that such freedom was a mere abstraction and that Sartre seemed to count unimportant the question of whether the person in his specific situation did or did not have scope for the creative life which his freedom would like to choose. And they complained that Sartre showed no understanding of the almost insuperable barriers which made astronomical the odds that a given person would actually make a new choice of his way of being. Today Sartre seems to agree with those critics. "The truth of a man is his work and his wages," he says. It is nonsense to talk of freedom when a man's only choice is between life on a subhuman scale and death. Furthermore, in the present world where there exist only societies based on exploitation, "everyone is lost since childhood." Where economic deprivation does not restrict freedom, the institutions of a class society do.

Sartre summarizes these ideas in a statement which, if taken by itself, might seem to deny everything he had written during the first half of his career. It occurs at the end of the section called "Marxism and Existentialism." Sartre quotes Marx's declaration to the effect that "the mode of production of material life generally dominates the development of social, political, and intellectual life." Sartre extends this to say that we cannot go beyond this "factual evidence" until transformed social relations and technical progress have freed humanity from the yoke of scarcity. Marx had said that the reign of freedom would begin only when the problem of material production had been fully met and solved. Sartre writes:

> As soon as there will exist *for everyone* a margin of *real* freedom beyond the production of life, Marxism will have lived out its span; a philosophy of freedom will take its place. But we have no means, no intellectual instrument, no concrete experience which allows us to conceive of this freedom or of this philosophy.[9]

It would be easy to conclude upon superficial reading that this is what all his critics insisted in the first place. Man's existential freedom doesn't amount to a pair of deuces when the chips are down. And if we can't even conceive of what a philosophy of freedom would be like, then what are we to make of existentialism? Is this Sartre's recantation? Was *Being and Nothingness* false or merely irrelevant? The statement certainly indicates a departure from what Sartre had led us to expect in 1943. At that time, in the concluding pages of *Being and Nothingness*, he implied that his next work would be an ethics. The *Critique* is not an ethics. Sartre evidently believes that so long as we live in a society based on falsehood and inequity, any individual ethics is at best a compromise. Both in order of importance and logically, social reorganization seems to Sartre to come first. He has always maintained that the source of values, upon which ethical conduct depends, must be the choice of the free individual or of many free persons working together. Where the value has not been

[9] *Search for a Method,* p. 34.

chosen by the person concerned, the ethical imperative that rests upon it can hardly be recognized as binding. Consequently, the ethics of a philosophy of freedom is not possible in a society where men are not free. It must be in some such sense that Sartre states that we cannot conceive of a philosophy of freedom. The statement seems to say also that for most people the necessary scope for creative living is lacking, that, for the moment, man's possession of psychological freedom is largely an abstraction and of little value in producing a life that is satisfying to the individual person.

Nevertheless, this same passage furnishes its own refutation for any idea that Sartre has renounced his earlier belief that man is radically free or that this fact of his freedom is the most explosively significant truth about him. Even as Sartre admits that we cannot claim that all men today possess "real freedom," he affirms the possibility that there will someday be a society in which scarcity will no longer be the determining factor, in which the true philosophy of freedom will be the only one suitable to men's needs. Neither the old-fashioned ideal of "progress" nor any supra-human dialectic assures the arrival of that time. But the dialectical movement of human beings consciously making their history in common *may* bring it about. Its actualization depends on the willingness of individuals to recognize existing contradictions and speed the creation of the resolving synthesis. Since Sartre rejects all belief in a mechanistic working out of history, he could not indicate the possibility of a future "philosophy of freedom" if he did not believe in freedom as a present reality in men—even if at present it exists more as an abstraction than in any practical form. The statement that we cannot conceive of its content is not a negative statement about man's potentialities, but rather the affirmation of the greatest, most far-reaching possibility of all—that man is free to transform himself, if he so choose, into a being so different that we cannot even in our imagination grasp what his creativity might demand or what might satisfy the new being he has made of himself.

Sartre states that the ultimate ideal for mankind would be a world in which all men worked together in full consciousness to make their history in common. We occasionally see a first approximation of this in what he calls the "group-in-fusion," a genuine "we-subject." Here individual *praxis* gives way to common *praxis*, and there emerges "the common individual." The term is somewhat horrifying, but Sartre does not mean by it a person who is stripped of all those qualities uniquely his and made like everyone else. "We are all brothers," he says, "but we are not like peas in a pod." [1] In the group-in-fusion there is no longer an I-you division or I-they. Rather it is a collection of "thirds" in which each third is a "myself" inasmuch as all are working to accomplish the same goal. The group achieves ends which are my ends but which I could not attain by myself. The aim of the group is to develop and to utilize those qualities and potentialities which are peculiar to each of its members. At present such groups are generally constituted only in the face of common danger and for the sake of immediate goals. Once the crisis is past, they tend to hold themselves together by sacred vows and by terror, for the danger of the disintegration of the group becomes the common danger which threatens them. At best the group crystallizes into an institution, whose heavy bureaucracy renders worse

[1] *Critique,* p. 453.

than ever man's damnation in the *pratico-inerte*. But Sartre does not feel that this outcome is inevitable. If the common end becomes the liberation of *all* men and if at long last all men join in writing the history of this liberation, then we may truthfully say that there is a single history of man; for this history would be both retrospectively and prospectively totalizing.

Sartre speaks not only of a history whose movement is both dialectical and totalizing but also of a single Truth of Man. Are we to understand that he identifies Truth with the dialectical movement itself or that—as one critic has said—he "is equating the cause of truth with that of the rising class"?[2] If one means by this that Sartre sets up some absolute, objective Truth, existing almost as an entity independently of the works of man, then the answer is clearly no. Yet he unquestionably relates the idea of truth to the dialectical interpretation of man. Because we have not yet constructed a new kind of rationality, he says,

> I state as a fact—absolutely no one, either in the East or in the West, writes or speaks a sentence or a word about us and our contemporaries that is not a gross error.[3]

What he means here first of all is probably that the logical forms and the language in which our thought is expressed are appropriate only for the objects of science and not for the free process which is man. He refers as well to the fact that our language has been designed to further the ideas of a society which through ignorance

[2] Philip Thody: *Jean-Paul Sartre: A Literary and Political Study* (London: Hamish Hamilton; 1960), p. 227. Despite minor disagreements with Mr. Thody, I think his discussion in Part Four, "Politics," is the best available presentation of the history of Sartre's political development.

[3] *Search for a Method*, p. 111.

or by design did not recognize the reality of the dialectical movement in history. In a note attached to this sentence Sartre goes a step further and identifies the false with that which is dead. One can find some truth —that is, something living—even in the midst of error. "Condillac's philosophy in his century, in the current which carried the bourgeoisie toward revolution and liberalism, was much more true—as a real factor in historical evolution—than Jaspers's philosophy is to-day." Sartre saves us from total confusion by adding the words "as a real factor in historical evolution." He does not quite say that a thing is true *absolutely* to the degree that it helps to further the Marxist goal. Nevertheless, the association of ideas cannot be denied.

I think it would be fair to Sartre if we were to give some such explanation as this: If it is true that man's only essence is his existential freedom, then the society and the language which treat him as if he were not free and prevent him from practically realizing his freedom are based on falsehood. If the movement of dialectical materialism (which means a historical materialism viewed dialectically) is to develop a society consistent with man's existential condition, then the interpretation of this movement is a dialectical truth. There would be many individual truths in a society capable of developing a philosophy of freedom, but there would be a totalizing truth as well. This truth would arise as the resolving synthesis of the most fundamental of all contradictions in man's situation—that he is free and that he is the prisoner of his own material image.

Erich Fromm calls Marx's philosophy "a spiritual existentialism in secular language." He justifies the appellation by pointing out that "Marx is primarily concerned with the emancipation of man as an individual, the overcoming of alienation, the restoration of his capacity to relate himself fully to man and to nature." [4] I do not think that Sartre could object to Fromm's formulation of Marx's essential aim. He is like Fromm, too, in refusing to identify Marxism either with the writings of post-Marxist theoreticians or with Communism as it has been institutionalized in the Soviet Union. But Sartre prefers to think of existentialism as the contributing ideology and of Marxism as the philosophy which at the present time we cannot go beyond. His aim is not to incorporate a modified Marxism into existentialism, but to hasten the moment at which existentialism may welcome its own dissolution into Marxism. It is easy to see why. Existentialism has been concerned with the individual's attempt to rediscover himself and his freedom and to learn how he might best commit his freedom. Stalinist Marxism, as Sartre sometimes calls it, suppressed the individual fully as much as Hegelianism, allowed him no more specifically "human" traits than behaviorist psychology. But a Marxism which has been de-Stalinized, which recognizes that it is still in its infancy, a Marxism which reinstates the individual and his *praxis* at the very heart of history— this seems to Sartre the proper place for an existentialist freedom to commit itself. A true Marxism will recognize that history is not necessarily and forever a history of human relations determined by scarcity. It will seek its own dissolution at that time when men and women will find that the image which their *praxis* has inscribed in the *pratico-inerte* is in truth the reflection of their freedom.

---

[4] *Marx's Concept of Man* (New York: Frederick Ungar; 1961), p. 5.

ACKNOWLEDGMENT

I SHOULD like to thank Gilberte and Donald Sutherland for their valuable help in tracking down the nuances of many a French word and phrase. I should like also to express my appreciation to Phyllis Berdt Kenevan, who read the translation and discussed it with me. Finally, I am grateful to the University of Colorado Council on Research and Creative Work, which furnished funds for the preparation of the manuscript.

HAZEL E. BARNES

Boulder, Colorado

❀❀❀❀❀❀❀❀❀❀❀❀❀❀❀❀❀❀❀❀❀❀❀❀❀❀❀❀❀

PREFACE

Search for a Method was written for a particular occasion, and this accounts for its slightly hybrid character. For this reason, too, the problems it raises seem always to be approached indirectly. A Polish review had decided to publish, during the winter of 1957, an issue devoted to French culture; it wanted to give to its readers a panoramic view of our intellectual groups, what we in France still call "our families of the mind." It invited the collaboration of a number of authors and proposed to me that I should deal with the subject "The Situation of Existentialism in 1957."

I do not like to talk about existentialism. It is the nature of an intellectual quest to be undefined. To name it and to define it is to wrap it up and tie the knot. What is left? A finished, already outdated mode of culture, something like a brand of soap—in other words, an idea. I would have refused the request of my Polish friends if I had not seen in the suggestion a means of expressing, in a country with a Marxist culture, the existing contradictions in its philosophy. Within this perspective, I believed that I could group the internal conflicts which split this philosophy, centering them on one principal opposition: that of existence and knowledge. Perhaps I would have been more direct if plans for the arrangement of the "French" number had not made it necessary for me to speak primarily about the existential ideology, just as a Marxist philosopher, Henri Lefebvre, was asked to "situate" the contradictions and the development of Marxism in France during these last years.

Some time later I reprinted my article in the review *Les Temps modernes*, altering it considerably so as to adapt it to the needs of French readers. This is the version which is published here. The essay, which originally was called *Existentialism and Marxism*, now has the title *Search for a Method*.

Finally, there is *one* question which I am posing— only one: Do we have today the means to constitute a structural, historical anthropology? It finds its place within Marxist philosophy because—as will be seen further on—I consider Marxism the one philosophy of our time which we cannot go beyond and because I hold the ideology of existence and its "comprehensive" method to be an enclave inside Marxism, which simultaneously engenders it and rejects it.

From Marxism, which gave it a new birth, the ideology of existence inherits two requirements which Marxism itself derives from Hegelianism: if such a thing as a Truth can exist in anthropology, it must be a truth that has *become*, and it must make itself a *totalization*. It goes without saying that this double requirement defines that movement of being and of knowing (or of comprehension) which since Hegel is called "dialectic." Also, in *Search for a Method* I have taken it for granted that such a totalization is perpetually in process as History and as historical Truth. Starting from this fundamental postulate, I have attempted to bring to light the internal conflicts of philosophical anthropology, and in certain cases I have been able to outline—upon the methodological ground which I have chosen—the provisional solutions of these difficulties.

JEAN-PAUL SARTRE

CONTENTS

SEARCH FOR A METHOD

❀❀❀❀❀❀❀❀❀❀❀❀❀❀❀❀❀❀❀❀❀❀❀❀❀❀❀

I · MARXISM

AND EXISTENTIALISM

PHILOSOPHY appears to some people as a homogeneous milieu: there thoughts are born and die, there systems are built, and there, in turn, they collapse. Others take *Philosophy* for a specific attitude which we can freely adopt at will. Still others see it as a determined segment of culture. In our view *Philosophy* does not exist. In whatever form we consider it, this shadow of science, this Gray Eminence of humanity, is only a hypostatized abstraction. Actually, there are *philosophies*. Or rather—for you would never at the same time find more than *one* living philosophy—under certain well-defined circumstances *a philosophy* is developed for the purpose of giving expression to the general movement of the society. So long as a philosophy is alive, it serves as a cultural milieu for its contemporaries. This disconcerting object presents itself *at the same time* under profoundly distinct aspects, the unification of which it is continually effecting.

A philosophy is first of all a particular way in which

the "rising" class becomes conscious of itself.[1] This consciousness may be clear or confused, indirect or direct. At the time of the *noblesse de robe* [2] and of mercantile capitalism, a bourgeoisie of lawyers, merchants, and bankers gained a certain self-awareness through Cartesianism; a century and a half later, in the primitive stage of industrialization, a bourgeoisie of manufacturers, engineers, and scientists dimly discovered itself in the image of universal man which Kantianism offered to it.

But if it is to be truly philosophical, this mirror must be presented as the totalization of contemporary Knowledge. The philosopher effects the unification of everything that is known, following certain guiding schemata which express the attitudes and techniques of the rising class regarding its own period and the world. Later, when the details of this Knowledge have been, one by one, challenged and destroyed by the advance of learning, the over-all concept will still remain as an undifferentiated content. These achievements of knowing, after having been first bound together by principles, will in turn—crushed and almost undecipherable—bind together the principles. Reduced to its simplest expression, the philosophical object will remain in "the objec-

[1] If I do not mention here the *person* who is objectified and revealed in his work, it is because the philosophy of a period extends far beyond the philosopher who first gave it shape—no matter how great he may be. But conversely we shall see that the study of particular doctrines is inseparable from a real investigation of philosophies. Cartesianism illuminates the period and *situates* Descartes within the totalitarian development of analytical reason; in these terms, Descartes, taken as a person and as a philosopher, clarifies the historical (hence the particular) meaning of the new rationality up to the middle of the eighteenth century.

[2] *Noblesse de robe* was originally the designation given in France to those members of the bourgeoisie who were awarded titles of nobility in recognition of outstanding achievement or services to the State. Later it was used more loosely to refer to any "new" nobility. H.B.

tive mind" in the form of a regulative Idea, pointing to an infinite task. Thus, in France one speaks of "the Kantian Idea" or in Germany of "Fichte's *Weltanschauung*." This is because a philosophy, when it is at the height of its power, is never presented as something inert, as the passive, already terminated unity of Knowledge. Born from the movement of society, it is itself a movement and acts upon the future. This concrete totalization is at the same time the abstract project of pursuing the unification up to its final limits. In this sense philosophy is characterized as a method of investigation and explication. The confidence which it has in itself and in its future development merely reproduces the certitudes of the class which supports it. Every philosophy is practical, even the one which at first appears to be the most contemplative. Its method is a social and political weapon. The analytical, critical rationalism of the great Cartesians has survived them; born from conflict, it looked back to clarify the conflict. At the time when the bourgeoisie sought to undermine the institutions of the Ancien Régime, it attacked the outworn significations which tried to justify them.[3] Later it gave service to liberalism, and it provided a doctrine for procedures that attempted to realize the "atomization" of the Proletariat.

Thus a philosophy remains efficacious so long as the *praxis* [4] which has engendered it, which supports it, and

[3] In the case of Cartesianism, the action of "philosophy" remains negative; it clears the ground, it destroys, and it enables men, across the infinite complexities and particularisms of the feudal system, to catch a glimpse of the abstract universality of bourgeois property. But under different circumstances, when the social struggle itself assumes other forms, the theory's contribution can be positive.

[4] The Greek word *praxis* means "deed" or "action." As Sartre uses it, *praxis* refers to any purposeful human activity. It is closely allied to the existential project which Sartre made so important a part of his philosophy in *Being and Nothingness*. H.B.

which is clarified by it, is still alive. But it is transformed, it loses its uniqueness, it is stripped of its original, dated content to the extent that it gradually im-
pregnates the masses so as to become in and through
them a collective instrument of emancipation. In this
way Cartesianism, in the eighteenth century, appears
under two indissoluble and complementary aspects. On
the one hand, as the Idea of reason, as an analytical
method, it inspires Holbach, Helvetius, Diderot, even
Rousseau; it is Cartesianism which we find at the source
of anti-religious pamphlets as well as of mechanistic
materialism. On the other hand, it passes into ano-
nymity and conditions the attitudes of the Third Estate.
In each case universal, analytical Reason vanishes and
reappears in the form of "spontaneity." This means that
the immediate response of the oppressed to oppression
will be *critical*. The abstract revolt precedes the French
Revolution and armed insurrection by some years. But
the directed violence of weapons will overthrow privileges which have already been dissolved in Reason.
Things go so far that the philosophical mind crosses
the boundaries of the bourgeoisie and infiltrates the
ranks of the populace. This is the moment at which the
French bourgeoisie claims that it is a universal class;
the infiltrations of its philosophy will permit it to mask
the struggles which are beginning to split the Third
Estate and will allow it to find a language and common
gestures for all revolutionary classes.

If philosophy is to be simultaneously a totalization of
knowledge, a method, a regulative Idea, an offensive
weapon, and a community of language, if this "vision
of the world" is also an instrument which ferments
rotten societies, if this particular conception of a man
or of a group of men becomes the culture and sometimes

the nature of a whole class—then it is very clear that the periods of philosophical creation are rare. Between the seventeenth century and the twentieth, I see three such periods, which I would designate by the names of the men who dominated them: there is the "moment" of Descartes and Locke, that of Kant and Hegel, finally that of Marx. These three philosophies become, each in its turn, the humus of every particular thought and the horizon of all culture; there is no going beyond them so long as man has not gone beyond the historical moment which they express. I have often remarked on the fact that an "anti-Marxist" argument is only the apparent rejuvenation of a pre-Marxist idea. A so-called "going beyond" Marxism will be at worst only a return to pre-Marxism; at best, only the rediscovery of a thought already contained in the philosophy which one believes he has gone beyond. As for "revisionism," this is either a truism or an absurdity. There is no need to readapt a living philosophy to the course of the world; it adapts itself by means of thousands of new efforts, thousands of particular pursuits, for the philosophy is one with the movement of society. Despite their good intentions, those very people who believe themselves to be the most faithful spokesmen for their predecessors transform the thoughts which they want simply to repeat; methods are modified because they are applied to new objects. If this movement on the part of the philosophy no longer exists, one of two things is true: either the philosophy is dead or it is going through a "crisis." In the first case there is no question of revising, but of razing a rotten building; in the second case the "philosophical crisis" is the particular expression of a social crisis, and its immobility is conditioned by the contradictions which split the society. A so-called "revision," performed by "experts," would be, therefore, only an idealist mystification without real significance. It is the very movement of History, the struggle of men on all planes and on all levels of human activity, which will set free captive thought and permit it to attain its full development.

Those intellectuals who come after the great flowering and who undertake to set the systems in order or to use the new methods to conquer territory not yet fully explored, those who provide practical applications for the theory and employ it as a tool to destroy and to construct—they should not be called philosophers. They cultivate the domain, they take an inventory, they erect certain structures there, they may even bring about certain internal changes; but they still get their nourishment from the living thought of the great dead. They are borne along by the crowd on the march, and it is the crowd which constitutes their cultural milieu and their future, which determines the field of their investigations, and even of their "creation." These *relative* men I propose to call "ideologists." [5] And since I am to speak of existentialism, let it be understood that I take it to be an "ideology." It is a parasitical system living on the margin of Knowledge, which at first it opposed but into which today it seeks to be integrated. If we are to understand its present ambitions and its function we must go back to the time of Kierkegaard.

The most ample philosophical totalization is Hegelianism. Here Knowledge is raised to its most eminent dignity. It is not limited to viewing Being from the outside; it incorporates Being and dissolves it in itself.

[5] Sartre's word is *idéologues*. I translate it "ideologists" after the analogy of words such as *philologue* (English "philologist"). H.B.

Mind objectifies itself, alienates itself, and recovers itself—without ceasing; it realizes itself through its own history. Man externalizes himself, he loses himself in things; but every alienation is surmounted by the absolute Knowledge of the philosopher. Thus those cleavages, those contradictions which cause our unhappiness are moments which are posited in order that they may be surpassed. We are not only *knowers;* in the triumph of intellectual self-consciousness, we appear as the *known.* Knowledge pierces us through and through; it situates us before dissolving us. We are integrated alive in the supreme totalization. Thus the pure, lived aspect of a tragic experience, a suffering unto death, is absorbed by the system as a relatively abstract determination which must be mediated, as a passage toward the Absolute, the only genuine concrete.[6]

---

[6] It is entirely possible, of course, to draw Hegel over to the side of existentialism, and Hyppolite endeavored to do so, not without success, in his *Studies in Marx and Hegel.* Was it not Hegel who first pointed out that "the appearance as such is a reality"? And is not his panlogicism complemented by a pantragicism? Can we not with good reason say that for Hegel "existences are enmeshed in the history which they make and which, as a concrete universality, is what judges and transcends them"? One can do this easily, but that is not the question. What Kierkegaard opposes in Hegel is the fact that for Hegel the tragedy of a particular life is always surpassed. The lived fades away into knowledge. Hegel talks to us about the slave and his fear of death. But the fear which was *felt* becomes the simple object of knowing, and the moment of a transformation which is itself surpassed. In Kierkegaard's view it is of no importance that Hegel speaks of "freedom to die" or that he correctly describes certain aspects of faith. What Kierkegaard complains of in Hegelianism is that it neglects the *unsurpassable opaqueness* of the lived experience. The disagreement is not only and not primarily at the level of concepts but rather has to do with the critique of knowledge and the delimitation of its scope. For example, it is perfectly correct to point out that Hegel is profoundly aware of the unity of life and consciousness and of the opposition between them. But it is also true that these are already recognized as incomplete *from the point of view of* the totality. Or, to use for the moment the terms of modern semeiology —for Hegel, the *Signifying* (at any moment of history) is the move-

Compared with Hegel, Kierkegaard scarcely seems to count. He is certainly not a philosopher; moreover, he himself refused this title. In fact, he is a Christian who is not willing to let himself be enclosed in the system and who, against Hegel's "intellectualism," asserts unrelentingly the irreducibility and the specificity of what is lived. There is no doubt, as Jean Wahl has remarked, that a Hegelian would have assimilated this romantic and obstinate consciousness to the "unhappy consciousness," a moment which had already been surpassed and known in its essential characteristics. But it is precisely this objective knowledge which Kierkegaard challenges. For him the surpassing of the unhappy consciousness remains purely verbal. The *existing* man cannot be assimilated by a system of ideas. Whatever one may say or think about suffering, it escapes knowledge to the extent that it is suffered in itself, for itself, and to the degree that knowledge remains powerless to transform it. "The philosopher constructs a palace of ideas and lives in a hovel." Of course, it is religion which Kierkegaard wants to defend. Hegel was not willing for Christianity to be "surpassed," but for this very reason he made it the highest moment of human existence. Kierkegaard, on the contrary, insists on the transcendence of the Divine; between man and God he puts an infinite distance. The existence of the Omnipotent cannot be the object of an objective knowledge; it becomes the aim of a subjective faith. And this faith, in turn, with its strength and its spontaneous

---

ment of Mind (which will be constituted as the signifying-signified and the signified-signifying; that is, as absolute-subject); the *Signified* is the living man and his objectification. For Kierkegaard, man is the Signifying; he himself produces the significations, and no signification points to him from outside (Abraham does not know whether he is Abraham); man is never the *signified* (not even by God).

affirmation, will never be reduced to a moment which can be surpassed and classified, to a knowing. Thus Kierkegaard is led to champion the cause of pure, unique subjectivity against the objective universality of essence, the narrow, passionate intransigence of the immediate life against the tranquil mediation of all reality, faith, which stubbornly asserts itself, against scientific evidence—*despite* the scandal. He looks everywhere for weapons to aid him in escaping from the terrible "mediation"; he discovers within himself oppositions, indecisions, equivocations which cannot be surpassed: paradoxes, ambiguities, discontinuities, dilemmas, etc. In all these inward conflicts, Hegel would doubtless see only contradictions in formation or in process of development—but this is exactly what Kierkegaard reproaches him for: even before becoming aware of them, the philosopher of Jena would have decided to consider them truncated ideas. In fact, the *subjective* life, just insofar as it is lived, can never be made the object of a knowledge. On principle it escapes knowing, and the relation of the believer to transcendence can only be conceived of in the form of a *going beyond*. This inwardness, which in its narrowness and its infinite depth claims to affirm itself against all philosophy, this subjectivity rediscovered beyond language as the personal adventure of each man in the face of others and of God —this is what Kierkegaard called *existence*.

We see that Kierkegaard is inseparable from Hegel, and that this vehement negation of every system can arise only within a cultural field entirely dominated by Hegelianism. The Dane feels himself hemmed in by concepts, by History, he fights for his life; it is the reaction of Christian romanticism against the rationalist humanization of faith. It would be too easy to reject this work as simply subjectivism; what we ought rather to point out, in placing it back within the framework of its period, is that Kierkegaard has as much right on his side as Hegel has on his. Hegel is right: unlike the Danish ideologist, who obstinately fixed his stand on poor, frozen paradoxes ultimately referring to an empty subjectivity, the philosopher of Jena aims through his concepts at the veritable concrete; for him, mediation is always presented as an enrichment. Kierkegaard is right: grief, need, passion, the pain of men, are brute realities which can be neither surpassed nor changed by knowledge. To be sure, Kierkegaard's religious subjectivism can with good reason be taken as the very peak of idealism; but in relation to Hegel, he marks a progress toward realism, since he insists above all on the *primacy* of the specifically real over thought, that the real cannot be reduced to thought. There are today some psychologists and psychiatrists [7] who consider certain evolutions of our inward life to be the result of a work which it performs upon itself. In this sense Kierkegaardian *existence* is the *work* of our inner life—resistances overcome and perpetually reborn, efforts perpetually renewed, despairs surmounted, provisional failures and precarious victories—and this work is directly opposed to intellectual knowing. Kierkegaard was perhaps the first to point out, against Hegel and thanks to him, the incommensurability of the real and knowledge. This incommensurability may be the origin of a conservative irrationalism; it is even one of the ways in which we may understand this ideologist's writings. But it can be seen also as the death of absolute idealism; ideas do not change men. Knowing the cause of a passion is not enough to overcome it; one must live it, one must oppose

[7] Cf. Lagache: *Le Travail du deuil* (*The Work of Mourning*).

other passions to it, one must combat it tenaciously, in short one must "work oneself over."

It is striking that Marxism addresses the same reproach to Hegel though from quite another point of view. For Marx, indeed, Hegel has confused objectification, the simple externalization of man in the universe, with the alienation which turns his externalization back against man. Taken by itself—Marx emphasizes this again and again—objectification would be an opening out; it would allow man, who produces and reproduces his life without ceasing and who transforms himself by changing nature, to "contemplate himself in a world which he has created." No dialectical sleight of hand can make alienation come out of it; this is why what is involved here is not a mere play of concepts but real History. "In the social production of their existence, men enter into relations which are determined, necessary, independent of their will; these relations of production correspond to a given stage of development of their material productive forces. The totality of these relations of production constitutes the real foundation upon which a legal and political superstructure arises and to which definite forms of social consciousness correspond." [8]

Now, in the present phase of our history, productive forces have entered into conflict with relations of production. Creative work is alienated; man does not recognize himself in his own product, and his exhausting labor appears to him as a hostile force. Since alienation comes about as the result of this conflict, it is a historical

[8] Sartre has not given the source for this important quotation. It comes from Marx's *"Preface* to Contribution to a Critique of Political Economy." I am indebted for the discovery to Erich Fromm, who quotes the passage in *Marx's Concept of Man* (New York: Frederick Ungar; 1961), p. 17. H.B.

reality and completely irreducible to an idea. If men
are to free themselves from it, and if their work is to
become the pure objectification of themselves, it is not
enough that "consciousness think itself"; there must be
material work and revolutionary *praxis*. When Marx
writes: "Just as we do not judge an individual by his
own idea of himself, so we cannot judge a . . . period
of revolutionary upheaval by its own self-consciousness,"
he is indicating the priority of action (work and social *praxis*) over *knowledge* as well as their hetero-
geneity. He too asserts that the human fact is irreducible to knowing, that it must *be lived* and *produced;*
but he is not going to confuse it with the empty subjectivity of a puritanical and mystified petite bourgeoisie. He makes of it the immediate theme of the
philosophical totalization, and it is the concrete man
whom he puts at the center of his research, that man
who is defined simultaneously by his needs, by the
material conditions of his existence, and by the nature
of his work—that is, by his struggle against things and
against men.

Thus Marx, rather than Kierkegaard or Hegel, is
right, since he asserts with Kierkegaard the specificity
of human *existence* and, along with Hegel, takes the
concrete man in his objective reality. Under these circumstances, it would seem natural if existentialism, this
idealist protest against idealism, had lost all usefulness
and had not survived the decline of Hegelianism.

In fact, existentialism suffered an eclipse. In the gen-
eral struggle which bourgeois thought leads against
Marxist dialectic, it gets its support from the post-
Kantians, from Kant himself, and from Descartes; it
never thinks of addressing itself to Kierkegaard. The
Dane will reappear at the beginning of the twentieth

century when people will take it into their heads to fight against Marxism by opposing to it pluralisms, ambiguities, paradoxes; that is, his revival dates back to the moment when for the first time bourgeois thought was reduced to being on the defensive. Between the two World Wars the appearance of a German existentialism certainly corresponds—at least in the work of Jaspers [9]—to a surreptitious wish to resuscitate the transcendent. Already—as Jean Wahl has pointed out —one could wonder if Kierkegaard did not lure his readers into the depths of subjectivity for the sole purpose of making them discover there the unhappiness of man without God. This trap would be quite in keeping with the "great solitary" who denied communication between human beings and who saw no way to influence his fellow man except by "indirect action."

Jaspers himself put his cards on the table. He has done nothing except to comment upon his master; his originality consists especially in putting certain themes into relief and in hiding others. The transcendent, for example, appears at first to be absent from his thought, which in fact is haunted by it. We are taught to catch a presentiment of the transcendent in our failures; it is their profound meaning. This idea is already found in Kierkegaard, but it is less emphasized since this Christian thinks and lives within the compass of a revealed religion. Jaspers, mute on Revelation, leads us back— through discontinuity, pluralism, and impotence—to the pure, formal subjectivity which is discovered and which discovers transcendence through its defeats. Success, indeed, as an *objectification,* would enable the person to inscribe himself in things and finally would compel him to surpass himself. The meditation on failure is

[9] The case of Heidegger is too complex for me to discuss here.

perfectly suited to a bourgeoisie which is partially de-Christianized but which regrets its past faith because it has lost confidence in its rationalist, positivist ideology. Kierkegaard already considered that every victory is suspect because it turns man away from himself. Kafka took up this Christian theme again in his *Journal*. And one can find a certain truth in the idea, since in a world of alienation the individual conqueror does not recognize himself in his victory and becomes its slave. But what is important to Jaspers is to derive from all this a subjective pessimism, which ultimately emerges as a theological optimism that dares not speak its name. The transcendent, indeed, remains veiled; it is attested only by its absence. One will never go beyond pessimism; one will have a presentiment of reconciliation while remaining at the level of an insurmountable contradiction and a total cleavage. This condemnation of dialectic is aimed no longer at Hegel, but at Marx. It is no longer the refusal of *Knowledge,* but the refusal of *praxis.* Kierkegaard was unwilling to play the role of a concept in the Hegelian system; Jaspers refuses to cooperate *as an individual* with the history which Marxists are making. Kierkegaard realized some progress over Hegel by affirming the *reality* of the lived; Jaspers regresses in the historical movement, for he flees from the real movement of *praxis* and takes refuge in an abstract subjectivity, whose sole aim is to achieve a certain inward *quality.*[1] This ideology of withdrawal expressed quite well only yesterday the attitude of a certain Germany fixed on its two defeats and that of a certain European bourgeoisie which wants to justify its privi-

---

[1] Jaspers gives the name "existence" to this quality which is at once immanent (since it extends throughout our lived subjectivity) and transcendent (since it remains beyond our reach).

leges by an aristocracy of the soul, to find refuge from its objectivity in an exquisite subjectivity, and to let itself be fascinated by an ineffable present so as not to see its future. Philosophically this soft, devious thought is only a survival; it holds no great interest. But it is one more existentialism which has developed at the margin of Marxism and not against it. It is Marx with whom we claim kinship, and Marx of whom I wish to speak now.

By its *actual* presence, a philosophy transforms the structures of Knowledge, stimulates ideas; even when it defines the practical perspectives of an exploited class, it polarizes the culture of the ruling classes and changes it. Marx wrote that the ideas of the dominant class are the dominant ideas. He is *absolutely* right. In 1925, when I was twenty years old, there was no chair of Marxism at the University, and Communist students were very careful not to appeal to Marxism or even to mention it in their examinations; had they done so, they would have failed. The horror of dialectic was such that Hegel himself was unknown to us. Of course, they allowed us to read Marx; they even advised us to read him; one had to know him "in order to refute him." But without the Hegelian tradition, without Marxist teachers, without any planned program of study, without the instruments of thought, our generation, like the preceding ones and like that which followed, was wholly ignorant of historical materialism.[2] On the other hand, they taught us Aristotelian and mathematical logic in great detail. It was at about this time that I read *Capital* and *German Ideology*. I found

[2] This explains why intellectual Marxists of my age (whether Communists or not) are such poor dialecticians; they have returned, without knowing it, to mechanistic materialism.

everything perfectly clear, and I really understood absolutely nothing. To understand is to change, to go beyond oneself. This reading did not change me. By contrast, what did begin to change me was the *reality* of Marxism, the heavy presence on my horizon of the masses of workers, an enormous, somber body which *lived* Marxism, which *practiced* it, and which at a distance exercised an irresistible attraction on petit bourgeois intellectuals. When we read this philosophy in books, it enjoyed no privilege in our eyes. A priest, who has just written a voluminous and very interesting work on Marx, calmly states in the opening pages: "It is possible to study [his] thought just as securely as one studies that of any other philosopher or any other sociologist."[3] That was exactly what we believed. So long as this thought appeared to us through written words, we remained "objective." We said to ourselves: "Here are the conceptions of a German intellectual who lived in London in the middle of the last century." But when it was presented as a real determination of the Proletariat and as the profound meaning of its acts —for itself and in itself—then Marxism attracted us irresistibly without our knowing it, and it put all our acquired culture out of shape. I repeat, it was not the idea which unsettled us; nor was it the condition of the worker, which we knew abstractly but which we had not experienced. No, it was the two joined together. It was—as we would have said then in our idealist jargon even as we were breaking with idealism —the Proletariat as the incarnation and vehicle of an idea. And I believe that we must here complete Marx's statement: When the rising class becomes conscious of itself, this self-consciousness acts at a distance upon

[3] Calvez: *La Pensée de Karl Marx* (Le Seuil).

intellectuals and makes the ideas in their heads dis-
integrate. We rejected the official idealism in the name
of "the tragic sense of life." [4] This Proletariat, far off,
invisible, inaccessible, but conscious and acting, furnished the proof—obscurely for most of us—that not
all conflicts had been resolved. We had been brought
up in bourgeois humanism, and this optimistic humanism was shattered when we vaguely perceived around
our town the immense crowd of "sub-men conscious of
their subhumanity." But we sensed this shattering in a
way that was still idealist and individualist.

At about that time, the writers whom we loved explained to us that existence is a *scandal*. What interested us, however, was real men with their labors and
their troubles. We cried out for a philosophy which
would account for everything, and we did not perceive
that it existed already and that it was precisely this
philosophy which provoked in us this demand. At that
time one book enjoyed a great success among us—
Jean Wahl's *Toward the Concrete*. Yet we were dis-
appointed by this "toward." The total concrete was
what we wanted to leave behind us; the absolute concrete was what we wanted to achieve. Still the work
pleased us, for it embarrassed idealism by discovering
in the universe paradoxes, ambiguities, conflicts, still
unresolved. We learned to turn pluralism (that concept of the Right) against the optimistic, monistic idealism of our professors—in the name of a Leftist thought
which was still ignorant of itself. Enthusiastically we
adopted all those doctrines which divided men into
watertight groups. "Petit bourgeois" democrats, we

---

[4] This phrase was made popular by the Spanish philosopher Miguel
de Unamuno. Of course, this tragic sense had nothing in common
with the true conflicts of our period.

rejected racism, but we liked to think that "primitive mentality," the universe of the child and the madman, remained entirely impenetrable to us. Under the influence of war and the Russian Revolution, we offered violence—only theoretically, of course—in opposition to the sweet dreams of our professors. It was a wretched violence (insults, brawls, suicides, murders, irreparable catastrophes) which risked leading us to fascism; but in our eyes it had the advantage of highlighting the contradictions of reality. Thus Marxism as "a philosophy which had become the world" wrenched us away from the defunct culture of a bourgeoisie which was barely subsisting on its past. We plunged blindly down the dangerous path of a pluralist realism concerned with man and things in their "concrete" existence. Yet we remained within the compass of "dominating ideas." Although we wanted to know man in his real life, we did not as yet have the idea of considering him first a worker who produces the conditions of his life. For a long time we confused the *total* and the *individual*. Pluralism, which had served us so well against M. Brunschvicg's idealism, prevented us from understanding the dialectical totalization. It pleased us to decry essences and artificially isolated types rather than to reconstitute the synthetic movement of a truth that had "become." Political events led us to employ the schema of the "class struggle" as a sort of grid, more convenient than veridical; but it took the whole bloody history of this half century to make us grasp the reality of the class struggle and to situate us in a split society. It was the war which shattered the worn structures of our thought—War, Occupation, Resistance, the years which followed. We wanted to fight at the side of the working class; we finally understood that the concrete is history and dialectical action. We had repudiated pluralist realism only to have found it again among the fascists, and we discovered the world.

Why then has "existentialism" preserved its autonomy? Why has it not simply dissolved in Marxism?

Lukacs believed that he had answered this question in a small book called *Existentialism and Marxism*. According to him, bourgeois intellectuals have been forced "to abandon the method of idealism while safeguarding its results and its foundations; hence the historical necessity of a 'third path' (between materialism and idealism) in actuality and in the bourgeois consciousness during the imperialistic period." I shall show later the havoc which this wish to conceptualize a priori has wrought at the center of Marxism. Here let us simply observe that Lukacs fails absolutely to account for the principal fact: we were convinced *at one and the same time* that historical materialism furnished the only valid interpretation of history and that existentialism remained the only concrete approach to reality. I do not pretend to deny the contradictions in this attitude. I simply assert that Lukacs does not even suspect it. Many intellectuals, many students, have lived and still live with the tension of this double demand. How does this come about? It is due to a circumstance which Lukacs knew perfectly well but which he could not at that time even mention: Marxism, after drawing us to it as the moon draws the tides, after transforming all our ideas, after liquidating the categories of our bourgeois thought, abruptly left us stranded. It did not satisfy our need to understand. In the particular situation in which we were placed, it no longer had anything new to teach us, because it had come to a stop.

Marxism stopped. Precisely because this philosophy

wants to change the world, because its aim is "philos-ophy-becoming-the-world," because it is and wants to be *practical*, there arose within it a veritable schism which rejected theory on one side and *praxis* on the other. From the moment the U.S.S.R., encircled and alone, undertook its gigantic effort at industrialization, Marxism found itself unable to bear the shock of these new struggles, the practical necessities and the mistakes which are always inseparable from them. At this period of withdrawal (for the U.S.S.R.) and of ebb tide (for the revolutionary proletariats), the ideology itself was subordinated to a double need: security (that is, unity) and the construction of socialism *inside* the U.S.S.R. Concrete thought must be born from *praxis* and must turn back upon it in order to clarify it, not by chance and without rules, but—as in all sciences and all techniques—in conformity with principles. Now the Party leaders, bent on pushing the integration of the group to the limit, feared that the free process of truth, with all the discussions and all the conflicts which it involves, would break the unity of combat; they reserved for themselves the right to define the line and to interpret the event. In addition, out of fear that the experience might not provide its own clarities, that it might put into question certain of their guiding ideas and might contribute to "weakening the ideological struggle," they put the doctrine out of reach. The separation of theory and practice resulted in transforming the latter into an empiricism without principles; the former into a pure, fixed knowledge. On the other hand, the economic planning imposed by a bureaucracy unwilling to recognize its mistakes became thereby a violence done to reality. And since the future production of a nation was determined in offices, often outside its own territory, this violence had as its counter-part an absolute idealism. Men and things had to yield to ideas—a priori; experience, when it did not verify the predictions, could only be wrong. Budapest's sub-way was real in Rakosi's head. If Budapest's subsoil did not allow him to construct the subway, this was because the subsoil was counter-revolutionary. Marx-ism, as a philosophical interpretation of man and of history, necessarily had to reflect the preconceptions of the planned economy.

This fixed image of idealism and of violence did ideal-istic violence to facts. For years the Marxist intellectual believed that he served his party by violating experi-ence, by overlooking embarrassing details, by grossly simplifying the data, and above all, by conceptualizing the event *before* having studied it. And I do not mean to speak only of Communists, but of all the others—fellow travelers, Trotskyites, and Trotsky sympathizers —for they have been *created* by their sympathy for the Communist Party or by their opposition to it. On November 4, 1956, at the time of the second Soviet intervention in Hungary, each group already had its mind made up before it possessed any information on the situation. It had decided in advance whether it was witnessing an act of aggression on the part of the Rus-sian bureaucracy against the democracy of Workers' Committees, with a revolt of the masses against the bureaucratic system, or with a counter-revolutionary attempt which Soviet moderation had known how to check. Later there was news, a great deal of news; but I have not heard it said that even one Marxist changed his opinion.

Among the interpretations which I have just men-tioned, there is one which shows the method in all its nakedness, that which reduces the facts in Hungary to a "Soviet act of aggression against the democracy of Workers' Committees." [5] It is obvious that the Workers' Committees are a democratic institution; one can even maintain that they bear within them the future of the socialist society. But this does not alter the fact that they did not exist in Hungary at the time of the first Soviet intervention; and their appearance during the Insurrection was much too brief and too troubled for us to be able to speak of an organized democracy. No matter. There were Workers' Committees; a Soviet intervention took place. Starting from there, Marxist idealism proceeds to two simultaneous operations: conceptualization and passage to the limit. They push the empirical notion to the perfection of the type, the germ to its total development. At the same time they reject the equivocal givens of experience; these could only lead one astray. We will find ourselves then in the presence of a typical contradiction between two Platonic ideas: on the one side, the wavering policy of the U.S.S.R. gave way to the rigorous and predictable action of that entity, "the Soviet Bureaucracy"; on the other side, the Workers' Committees disappeared before that other entity, "the direct Democracy." I shall call these two objects "general particularities"; they are made to pass for particular, historical realities when we ought not to see in them anything more than the purely formal unity of abstract, universal relations. The process of making them into fetishes will be complete when each one is endowed with real powers: the Democracy of Workers' Committees holds within itself the absolute negation of the Bureaucracy, which reacts by crushing its adversary.

[5] Maintained by former Trotskyites.

Now there can be no doubt that the fruitfulness of living Marxism stemmed in part from its way of approaching experience. Marx was convinced that facts are never isolated appearances, that if they come into being together, it is always within the higher unity of a whole, that they are bound to each other by internal relations, and that the presence of one profoundly modifies the nature of the other. Consequently, Marx approached the study of the revolution of February 1848 or Louis Napoleon Bonaparte's *coup d'état* with a synthetic intent; he saw in these events totalities produced and at the same time split apart by their internal contradictions. Of course, the physicist's hypothesis, before it has been confirmed by experimentation, is also an interpretation of experience; it rejects empiricism simply because it is mute. But the constitutive schema of this hypothesis is universalizing, not totalizing. It determines a relation, a function, and not a concrete totality. The Marxist approaches the historical process with universalizing and totalizing schemata. Naturally the totalization was not made by chance. The theory had determined the choice of perspective and the order of the conditioning factors; it studied each particular process within the framework of a general system in evolution. But in no case, in Marx's own work, does this putting in perspective claim to prevent or to render useless the appreciation of the process as a *unique* totality. When, for example, he studies the brief and tragic history of the Republic of 1848, he does not limit himself—as would be done today—to stating that the republican petite bourgeoisie betrayed its ally, the Proletariat. On the contrary, he tries to account for this tragedy in its detail and in the aggregate. If he subordinates anecdotal facts to the totality (of a movement, of an attitude), he also seeks to discover the totality by means of the facts. In other words, he gives to each event, in addition to its particular signification, the role of being revealing. Since the ruling principle of the inquiry is the search for the synthetic ensemble, each fact, once established, is questioned and interpreted as part of a whole. It is on the basis of *the fact*, through the study of its lacks and its "oversignifications," that one determines, by virtue of a hypothesis, the totality at the heart of which the fact will recover its truth. Thus living Marxism is heuristic; its principles and its prior knowledge appear as regulative in relation to its concrete research. In the work of Marx we never find entities. Totalities (e.g., "the petite bourgeoisie" of the *18 Brumaire*) are living; they furnish their own definitions within the framework of the research.[6] Otherwise we could not understand the impor-

[6] The concept of "the petite bourgeoisie" exists in Marxist philosophy, of course, well before the study of Louis Napoleon's *coup d'état*. But this is because the petite bourgeoisie itself had already existed as a class for a long time. What is important is the fact that it evolves with history and that in 1848 it presents unique characteristics which the concept cannot derive from itself. We will see that Marx goes back to the general traits which defined it as a class and at the same time —in those terms and in the light of experience—he determines the specific traits which determined it as a unique reality in 1848. To take another example, see how he tries in 1853, in a series of articles (*The British Rule in India*), to portray the peculiar quality of Hindustan. Maximilien Rubel in his excellent book quotes this curious passage (so shocking to our contemporary Marxists). "This strange combination of Italy and Ireland, of a world of pleasure and a world of suffering, is anticipated in the old religious traditions of Hindustan, in that religion of sensual exuberance and savage asceticism . . ." (Rubel: *Karl Marx*, p. 302. The quotation from Marx appeared June 25, 1853, under the title *On India*.) Certainly we can find behind these words the true concepts and method: the social structure and the geographical aspect—that is what recalls Italy; English colonization—that is what recalls Ireland; etc. No matter. He gives a *reality* to these words—pleasure, suffering, sensual exuberance, and savage asceticism. Better yet, he shows the actual situation of Hindu-

tance which Marxists attach (even today) to "the analysis" of a situation. It goes without saying that this analysis is not enough and that it is but the first moment in an effort at synthetic reconstruction. But it is apparent also that the analysis is indispensable to the later reconstruction of the total structures.

Marxist voluntarism, which likes to speak of analysis, has reduced this operation to a simple ceremony. There is no longer any question of studying facts within the general perspective of Marxism so as to enrich our understanding and to clarify action. Analysis consists solely in getting rid of detail, in forcing the signification of certain events, in denaturing facts or even in inventing a nature for them in order to discover it later underneath them, as their substance, as unchangeable, fetishized "synthetic notions." The open concepts of Marxism have closed in. They are no longer *keys,* interpretive schemata; they are posited for themselves as an already totalized knowledge. To use Kantian terms— Marxism makes out of these particularized, fetishized types, constitutive concepts of experience. The real content of these typical concepts is always *past Knowledge;* but today's Marxist makes of it an eternal knowledge. His sole concern, at the moment of analysis, will be to "place" these entities. The more he is convinced that they represent truth a priori, the less fussy he will be about proof. The Kerstein Amendment, the appeals of Radio Free Europe, rumors—these are sufficient for the French Communists to "place" the entity "world imperialism" at the origin of the events in Hungary.

---

stan "anticipated" (*before the English*) by its old religious traditions. Whether Hindustan is actually this or something else matters little to us; what counts here is the synthetic view which *gives life* to the objects of the analysis.

The totalizing investigation has given way to a Scholasticism of the totality. The heuristic principle—"to search for the whole in its parts"—has become the terrorist practice [7] of "liquidating the particularity." It is not by chance that Lukacs—Lukacs who so often violates history—has found in 1956 the best definition of this frozen Marxism. Twenty years of practice give him all the authority necessary to call this pseudophilosophy *a voluntarist idealism.*

Today social and historical experience falls outside of Knowledge. Bourgeois concepts just manage to revive and quickly break down; those which survive lack any foundation. The real attainments of American Sociology cannot hide its theoretic uncertainty. Psychoanalysis, after a spectacular beginning, has stood still. It knows a great many details, but it lacks any firm foundation. Marxism possesses theoretical bases, it embraces all human activity; but it no longer *knows* anything. Its concepts are *dictates;* its goal is no longer to increase what it knows but to be itself constituted a priori as an absolute Knowledge. In view of this twofold ignorance, existentialism has been able to return and to maintain itself because it reaffirmed the reality of men as Kierkegaard asserted his own reality against Hegel. However, the Dane rejected the Hegelian conception of man and of the real. Existentialism and Marxism, on the contrary, aim at the same object; but Marxism has reabsorbed man into the idea, and existentialism seeks him everywhere *where he is,* at his work, in his home, in the street. We certainly do not claim—as Kierkegaard did —that this real man is unknowable. We say only that he is not known. If for the time being he escapes Knowl-

---

[7] At one time this intellectual terror corresponded to "the physical liquidation" of particular people.

edge, it is because the only concepts at our disposal for understanding him are borrowed either from the idealism of the Right or from the idealism of the Left. We are careful not to confuse these two idealisms: the former merits its name by the *content* of its concepts, and the latter by the *use* which today it makes of its concepts. It is true also that among the masses Marxist *practice* does not reflect, or only slightly reflects, the sclerosis of its theory. But it is precisely the conflict between revolutionary action and the Scholastic justification of this action which prevents Communist man—in socialist countries as in bourgeois countries—from achieving any clear self-consciousness. One of the most striking characteristics of our time is the fact that history is made without self-awareness. No doubt someone will say this has always been the case; and this was true up until the second half of the last century—that is, until Marx. But what has made the force and richness of Marxism is the fact that it has been the most radical attempt to clarify the historical process in its totality. For the last twenty years, on the contrary, its shadow has obscured history; this is because it has ceased to live *with history* and because it attempts, through a bureaucratic conservatism, to reduce change to identity.[8]

[8] I have already expressed my opinion on the Hungarian tragedy, and I shall not discuss the matter again. From the point of view of what concerns us here, it matters little a priori that the Communist commentators believed that they had to justify the Soviet intervention. What is really heart-breaking is the fact that their "analyses" totally suppressed the originality of the Hungarian fact. Yet there is no doubt that an insurrection at Budapest a dozen years after the war, less than five years after the death of Stalin, must present very particular characteristics. What do our "schematizers" do? They lay stress on the faults of the Party but without defining them. These indeterminate faults assume an abstract and eternal character which wrenches them from the historical context so as to make of them a

Yet we must be clear about all this. This sclerosis does not correspond to a normal aging. It is produced by a world-wide combination of circumstances of a particular type. Far from being exhausted, Marxism is still very young, almost in its infancy; it has scarcely begun to develop. It remains, therefore, the philosophy of our time. We cannot go beyond it because we have not gone beyond the circumstances which engendered it. Our thoughts, whatever they may be, can be formed only upon this humus; they must be contained within the framework which it furnishes for them or be lost in the void or retrogress. Existentialism, like Marxism, addresses itself to experience in order to discover there concrete syntheses; it can conceive of these syntheses only within a moving, dialectical totalization which is nothing else but history or—from the strictly cultural point of view which we have adopted here—"philosophy-becoming-the-world." For us, truth is something which becomes, it *has* and *will have* become. It is a totalization which is forever being totalized. Particular facts do not signify anything; they are neither true nor false so long as they are not related, through the media-

---

universal entity; it is "human error." The writers indicate the presence of reactionary elements, but without showing their Hungarian *reality*. Suddenly these reactionaries pass over into eternal Reaction; they are brothers of the counter-revolutionaries of 1793, and their only distinctive trait is the will to injure. Finally, those commentators present world imperialism as an inexhaustible, formless force, whose essence does not vary regardless of its point of application. They construct an interpretation which serves as a skeleton key to everything —out of three ingredients: errors, the local-reaction-which-profits-from-popular-discontent, and the exploitation-of-this-situation-by-world-imperialism. This interpretation can be applied as well or as badly to all insurrections, including the disturbances in Vendée or at Lyon in 1793, by merely putting "aristocracy" in place of "imperialism." In short, nothing new has happened. That is what had to be demonstrated.

tion of various partial totalities, to the totalization in process.

Let us go further. We agree with Garaudy when he writes (*Humanité*, May 17, 1955): "Marxism forms today the system of coordinates which alone permits it to situate and to define a thought in any domain whatsoever—from political economy to physics, from history to ethics." And we should agree all the more readily if he had extended his statement (but this was not his subject) to the actions of individuals and masses, to specific works, to modes of life, to labor, to feelings, to the particular evolution of an institution or a character. To go further, we are also in full agreement with Engels when he wrote in that letter which furnished Plekhanov the occasion for a famous attack against Bernstein: "There does not exist, as one would like to imagine now and then, simply for convenience, any effect produced automatically by the economic situation. On the contrary, it is men themselves who make their history, but within a given environment which conditions them and on the basis of real, prior conditions among which economic conditions—no matter how much influenced they may be by other political and ideological conditions—are nevertheless, in the final analysis, the determining conditions, constituting from one end to the other the guiding thread which alone puts us in a position to understand." It is already evident that we do not conceive of economic conditions as the simple, static structure of an unchangeable society; it is the contradictions within them which form the driving force of history. It is amusing that Lukacs, in the work which I have already quoted, believed he was distinguishing himself from us by recalling that Marxist definition of materialism: "the primacy of existence over conscious-

ness"—whereas existentialism, as its name sufficiently
indicates, makes of this primacy the object of its fundamental affirmation.[9]

[9] The *methodological* principle which holds that certitude begins
with reflection in no way contradicts the *anthropological* principle
which defines the concrete person by his materiality. For us, reflection
is not reduced to the simple immanence of idealist subjectivism; it is
a point of departure only if it throws us back immediately among
things and men, in the world. The only theory of knowledge which
can be valid today is one which is founded on that truth of microphysics: the experimenter is a part of the experimental system. This is
the only position which allows us to get rid of all idealist illusion, the
only one which shows the real man in the midst of the real world. But
this realism necessarily implies a reflective point of departure; that is,
the *revelation* of a situation is effected in and through the *praxis*
which changes it. We do not hold that this first act of becoming conscious of the situation is the originating source of an action; we
see in it a necessary moment of the action itself—the action, *in the
course of its accomplishment,* provides its own clarification. That does
not prevent this clarification from appearing in and by means of the
attainment of awareness on the part of the agents; and this in turn
necessarily implies that one must develop a theory of consciousness.
Yet the theory of knowledge continues to be the weak point in
Marxism. When Marx writes: "The materialist conception of the world
signifies simply the conception of nature as it is without any foreign
addition," he makes himself into an *objective observation* and claims
to contemplate nature as it is absolutely. Having stripped away all
subjectivity and having assimilated himself into pure objective truth,
he walks in a world of objects inhabited by object-men. By contrast, when Lenin speaks of our consciousness, he writes: "Consciousness is only the reflection of being, at best an approximately accurate
reflection"; and by a single stroke he removes from himself the right to
write what he is writing. In both cases it is a matter of suppressing
subjectivity: with Marx, we are placed beyond it; with Lenin, on this
side of it.

These two positions contradict each other. How can the "approximately accurate reflection" become the source of *materialistic rationalism?* The game is played on two levels: there is in Marxism a constituting consciousness which asserts a priori the rationality of the
world (and which, consequently, falls into idealism); this constituting
consciousness determines the constituted consciousness of particular
men as a simple reflection (which ends up in a skeptical idealism).
Both of these conceptions amount to breaking man's real relation
with history, since in the first, knowing is pure theory, a non-situated
observing, and in the second, it is a simple passivity. In the latter there
is no longer any experimenting, there is only a skeptical empiricism;
man vanishes and Hume's challenge is not taken up. In the former

To be still more explicit, we support unreservedly that formulation in *Capital* by which Marx means to define his "materialism": "The mode of production of

the experimenter transcends the experimental system. And let no one try to tie one to the other by a "dialectical theory of the reflection"; the two concepts are essentially *anti-dialectical*. When knowing is made apodictic, and when it is constituted against all possible questioning without ever defining its scope or its rights, then it is cut off from the world and becomes a formal system. When it is reduced to a pure psycho-physiological determination, it loses its primary quality, which is its relation to the object, in order to become itself a pure object of knowing. No mediation can link Marxism as a declaration of principles and apodictic truths to psycho-physiological reflection (or "dialectic"). These two conceptions of knowing (dogmatism and the knowing-dyad) are both of them *pre-Marxist*. In the movement of Marxist "analyses" and especially in the process of totalization, just as in Marx's remarks on the *practical* aspect of truth and on the general relations of theory and *praxis*, it would be easy to discover the rudiments of a *realistic* epistemology which has never been developed. But what we can and ought to construct on the basis of these scattered observations is a theory which *situates* knowing *in the world* (as the theory of the reflection attempts awkwardly to do) and which determines it in its *negativity* (that negativity which Stalinist dogmatism pushes to the absolute and which it transforms into a negation). Only then will it be understood that knowing is not a knowing of ideas but a practical knowing *of things;* then it will be possible to suppress the *reflection* as a useless and misleading intermediary. Then we will be able to account for the thought which is lost and alienated in the course of action so that it may be rediscovered by and in the action itself. But what are we to call this situated negativity, as a moment of *praxis* and as a pure relation to things themselves, if not exactly "consciousness"?

There are two ways to fall into idealism: The one consists of dissolving the real in subjectivity; the other in denying all real subjectivity in the interests of objectivity. The truth is that subjectivity is neither everything nor nothing; it represents a moment in the objective process (that in which externality is internalized), and this moment is perpetually eliminated only to be perpetually reborn. Now, each of these ephemeral moments—which rise up in the course of human history and which are never either the first or the last—is lived as a *point of departure* by the subject of history. "Class-consciousness" is not the simple lived contradiction which objectively characterizes the class considered; it is that contradiction already surpassed by *praxis* and thereby preserved and denied all at once. But it is precisely this revealing negativity, this distance within immediate proximity, which simultaneously constitutes what existentialism calls "consciousness *of* the object" and "non-thetic self-consciousness."

material life generally dominates the development of
social, political, and intellectual life." We cannot conceive of this conditioning in any form except that of a
dialectical movement (contradictions, surpassing, to-
talizations). M. Rubel criticizes me for not making any
allusion to this "Marxist materialism" in the article I
wrote in 1946, "Materialism and Revolution." [1] But he
himself supplies the reason for this omission. "It is true
that this author is directing his comments at Engels
rather than at Marx." Yes, and even more at contemporary French Marxists. But Marx's statement seems
to me to point to a factual evidence which we cannot go
beyond *so long as* the transformations of social relations and technical progress have not freed man from
the yoke of scarcity. We are all acquainted with the
passage in which Marx alludes to that far-off time:
"This reign of freedom does not begin in fact until the
time when the work imposed by necessity and external
finality shall cease; it is found, therefore, beyond the
sphere of material production proper" (*Capital*, III,
p. 873). As soon as there will exist *for everyone* a
margin of *real* freedom beyond the production of life,
Marxism will have lived out its span; a philosophy of
freedom will take its place. But we have no means, no
intellectual instrument, no concrete experience which
allows us to conceive of this freedom or of this philosophy.

[1] "Matérialisme et révolution," *Les Temps modernes*, Vol. I, Nos. 9
and 10 (June–July 1946). The article has been translated into English
by Annette Michelson and is included in Jean-Paul Sartre's *Literary
and Philosophical Essays* (New York: Criterion Books; 1955). H.B.

◦◦◦◦◦◦◦◦◦◦◦◦◦◦◦◦◦◦◦◦◦◦◦◦◦◦◦◦◦

II · THE PROBLEM

OF MEDIATIONS

AND AUXILIARY DISCIPLINES

WHY, THEN, are we not simply Marxists? It is because we take the statements of Engels and Garaudy as guiding principles, as indications of jobs to be done, as problems—not as concrete truths. It is because their assertions seem to us insufficiently defined and, as such, capable of numerous interpretations; in a word, it is because they appear to us as regulative ideas. The contemporary Marxist, on the contrary, finds them clear, precise, and unequivocal; for him they *already* constitute a *knowledge*. We think, on the other hand, that everything remains to be done; we must find the method and constitute the science.

Of course, Marxism allows us to *situate* a speech by Robespierre, the policy of the Montagnards with regard to the *sans-culottes*, the economic regulations and the laws concerning "price ceilings" voted by the Convention, as well as Valéry's *Poems* or *La Légende des siècles*. But just what is this *situating?* If I turn to the works of contemporary Marxists, I see that they mean to determine for the object considered its real place in the total process; they will establish the material conditions of its existence, the class which has produced it, the interests of that class (or of a segment of that class), its movement, the forms of its struggle against the other classes, the relation of forces to each other, the stakes, etc. The speech, the vote, the political action, or the book will appear then in its objective reality as a certain moment in this conflict. It will be defined in terms of the factors on which it depends and by the real action which it exerts; thereby it will be made to enter—as an exemplary manifestation—into the universality of the ideology or of the policy, which are themselves considered as superstructures. Thus the Girondists will be situated in reference to a bourgeoisie of merchants and shipowners who provoked war out of mercantile imperialism and who almost immediately wanted to stop it because it was injuring foreign trade. Marxists will, on the other hand, see in the Montagnards the representatives of a more recent bourgeoisie, enriched by buying up national properties and furnishing war materials, whose principal interest was consequently to prolong the conflict. Thus they will interpret the acts and discourses of Robespierre in terms of a fundamental economic contradiction: in order to continue the war, this petit bourgeois had to get his support from the people, but the fall of the assignat,[1] monopoly, and the shortage of food supplies led the people to demand an economic control which was injurious to the

[1] Paper money issued by the French Revolutionary Government after 1790. H.B.

interests of the Montagnards and repugnant to their liberal ideology. Behind this conflict we discover the most profound contradiction between authoritarian parliamentarianism and direct democracy.[2] Or suppose we want to situate one of today's authors? Idealism is the nourishing soil of all bourgeois productions; it is an active force, since it reflects in its own way the profound contradictions of society. Each of its concepts is a weapon against the rising ideology—the weapon is offensive or defensive according to circumstances; or, better yet, offensive at the start, it subsequently becomes defensive. Thus Lukacs will distinguish between the false calm of the early prewar period, which is expressed "by a sort of permanent carnival of fetishized interiority," and the great penitence, the ebb tide of the postwar period, in which writers seek "the third path" to disguise their idealism.

This method does not satisfy us. It is a priori. It does not derive its concepts from experience—or at least not from the new experiences which it seeks to interpret. It has already formed its concepts; it is already certain of their truth; it will assign to them the role of constitutive schemata. Its sole purpose is to force the events, the persons, or the acts considered into prefabricated molds. Consider Lukacs. For him, Heidegger's existentialism is changed into an activism under the influence of the Nazis; French existentialism, which is liberal and anti-fascist, expresses, on the contrary, the revolt of the petits bourgeois who were en-

---

[2] These comments and those which follow were suggested to me by Daniel Guérin's *La Lutte des classes sous la première République,* a work which is often open to question but fascinating and rich in new insights. Despite all the mistakes (due to Guérin's wish to force history), it remains one of the few *enriching* contributions that contemporary Marxists have made to the study of history.

slaved during the Occupation. What a beautiful fiction! Unfortunately he overlooks two essential facts. First, there existed in Germany *at least one* existentialist movement which refused all collusion with Hitlerism and which nevertheless survived until the Third Reich —that of Jaspers. Why did this undisciplined movement not conform to the schema imposed upon it? Could it have had, like Pavlov's dog, a "freedom-reflex"? Second, there is one essential factor in philosophy—time. One needs a great deal of it to write a theoretical work. My book *Being and Nothingness,* to which he refers directly, was the result of study begun in 1930. I read Husserl, Scheler, Heidegger, and Jaspers for the first time in 1933 during a year's residence at the French House in Berlin. It was *at this very moment* (when Heidegger should have been at the height of his "activism") that I was subjected to the influence of these writers. Finally, by the winter of 1939–40 I had already worked out my method and my principal conclusions. And what is this "activism" if not a formal, empty concept, permitting one to liquidate all at once a certain number of ideological systems which have only superficial resemblances to one another. Heidegger has *never* been an "activist"—at least not as he has expressed himself in his philosophical works. The very word, vague as it is, testifies to the total inability of the Marxist to comprehend any other thought. Yes, Lukacs has the instruments to understand Heidegger, but he will not understand him; for Lukacs would have to *read* him, to grasp the meaning of the sentences one by one. And there is no longer any Marxist, to my knowledge, who is still capable of doing this.[3] Finally, there

---

[3] This is because they insist on standing in their own light. They reject the hostile sentence (out of fear or hate or laziness) at the very

has existed a whole dialectic—and a very complex one
—from Brentano to Husserl and from Husserl to
Heidegger: influences, oppositions, agreements, new
oppositions, misunderstandings, distortions, denials,
surpassings, etc. All this adds up to what one could call
an *area history*. Ought we to consider it a pure epi-
phenomenon? According to what Lukacs says, yes. Or
does there exist some kind of movement of ideas, and
does Husserl's phenomenology—as a moment preserved
and surpassed—enter into Heidegger's system? In this
case the principles of Marxism are not changed, but the
situation becomes much more complex.

In the same way the desire to effect as quickly as
possible the reduction of the political to the social has
sometimes falsified Guérin's analyses. One can, with
some difficulty, grant with him that the revolutionary
war became, starting in 1789,[4] a new episode in the
commercial rivalry between the British and the French.
The bellicosity of the Girondists was essentially *political;* and doubtless, the Girondists expressed in their
policy the class which had produced them and the
interests of the milieu which supported them. Their dis-
dainful ideal, their wish to submit the populace whom
they despised to the enlightened elite of the bourgeoisie
(that is, to confer upon the bourgeoisie the role of enlightened despot), their verbal radicalism and their
practical opportunism, their sensibility, their careless-

---

moment that they want to open themselves to it. This contradiction
blocks them. They literally do not understand a word of what they
read. And I blame them for this lack of comprehension, not in the
name of some sort of bourgeois objectivity, but in the name of Marxism
itself. They will be able to reject and condemn more precisely, to
refute more triumphantly, exactly insofar as they first know what it is
that they are damning and refuting.

[4] Sartre's text has " '39," but this is clearly a misprint. H.B.

ness—all this bears a trademark. But what is expressed in this way is the intoxication of an intellectual petite bourgeoisie in the process of taking over power rather than the proud and already old-fashioned prudence of shipowners and merchants.

When Brissot threw France into war in order to save the Revolution and to unmask the treason of the king, this naïve Machiavellianism expressed perfectly in its turn the Girondist attitude which we have just described.[5] But if we put ourselves back in that period and if we consider what occurred just prior to these events: the king's flight, the massacre of the Republicans at the Champ-de-Mars, the shift to the Right on the part of the moribund Constituent Assembly and the revision of the Constitution, the uncertainty of the masses, who were disgusted with the monarchy and intimidated by repression, the massive abstention on the part of the Parisian bourgeoisie (10,000 voters as compared with 80,000 for the municipal elections), in a word, the

[5] One must not forget, however, that Robespierre, a Montagnard, supported Brissot's proposals up until the first days of December 1791. Even more, his synthetic intention increased the severity of the decrees which were put to the vote, because he was going straight to the essential. On November 28 he demanded that they neglect "the small powers" and address themselves directly to the Emperor, putting the matter to him in these terms: "We call upon you to disband [the assembled armies], or we declare war on you." It is important, too, that he changed his opinion very little under the influence of Billaud-Varennes (who insistently pointed out to the Jacobins the power of the *internal* enemies and the disastrous state of our defenses at the frontiers). It appears that Billaud's arguments took on their real meaning in Robespierre's eyes when he learned of the appointment of the Comte de Narbonne to the Ministry of War. From there on the conflict appeared to him to be a cleverly prepared trap, an infernal machine; at that point he abruptly grasped the dialectical connection between the external enemy and the internal enemy. The Marxist ought not to overlook these so-called "details"; they show that the immediate move of all the politicians was to declare war or at least to risk it. Below the surface the opposite move began to take shape at once, but its origin was not the wish for peace; it was *defiance*.

breakdown of the Revolution; and if we take into account also the Girondist ambitions, is there really any need to be in a hurry to cancel out *political praxis?* Must we recall the words of Brissot, "We have need of great treasons"? Must we insist on the precautions taken during the year 1792 to keep England out of a war which, according to Guérin, ought to be directed against her? [6] Is it indispensable to consider this enterprise an insubstantial appearance, disguising the conflict of economic interests, when by itself it proclaims its meaning and its goal—through contemporary speeches and writing? A historian—even a Marxist—cannot forget that the political reality for the men of 1792 is an absolute, an irreducible. To be sure, they commit the error of ignoring the action of other forces, more muffled, less clearly discernible, infinitely more powerful. But that is exactly what defines these men as the bourgeois of 1792. Is this any reason to commit the opposite error and to refuse to grant a relative irreducibility to their action and to the political motives which it defines?

There is no question here of determining, once and

---

[6] Let us recall that even after the decree of December 15, 1792, the hesitation and caution continued. Brissot and the Girondists did what they could to prevent the invasion of Holland; the banker Clavière (a friend of the followers of Brissot) opposed the idea of introducing the assignats into occupied countries. Debry proposed to declare that the nation was no longer in danger and to recall all the measures which public safety had imposed. The Girondists were well aware that the war was forcing a policy that was more and more democratic, and this is what they were afraid of. But the party found itself cornered; it was reminded each day that it was responsible for having declared war. In fact, the decree of December 15 did have an economic purpose, but it was one which involved, if I may say so, a continental economy—to make the conquered countries bear the expenses of the war. Thus the economic aspect (and a disastrous one) of the war with England did not appear until 1793, when the die was already cast.

for all, the nature and the force of the resistance which the phenomena of superstructure oppose to all attempts at ruthless reduction; this would be to oppose one idealism to another. What is necessary is simply to reject apriorism. The unprejudiced examination of the historical object will be able by itself to determine in each case whether the action or the work reflects the superstructural motives of groups or of individuals formed by certain basic conditionings, or whether one can explain them only by referring immediately to economic contradictions and to conflicts of material interests. The American Civil War, despite the Puritan idealism of the Northerners, must be interpreted directly in economic terms; the people of that time were themselves aware of it. The French Revolution, on the other hand, although by 1793 it had assumed a very precise economic sense, is not *directly reducible* in 1792 to the age-old conflict of mercantile capitalisms. It must first be made to pass through a process of mediation, one which will bring into play the concrete men who were involved in it, the specific character it took on from its basic conditioning, the ideological instruments it employed, the real environment of the Revolution. Above all, we must not forget that the political theory *by itself* had a social and economic meaning, since the bourgeoisie was struggling against the bonds of an ancient feudalism which *from within* prevented it from realizing its full development. In the same way it is absurd to be *too quick* in reducing all ideological generosity to class interests. One ends up by proving that those anti-Marxists whom today we call "Machiavellians" are right. There is no doubt that, when the Legislative Assembly decided to undertake a war of liberation, it launched itself forward into a complex historical process which would necessarily lead it to waging wars of conquest. But it would be a poor Machiavellian who would reduce the ideology of 1792 to the role of a simple cover-up for bourgeois imperialism. If we do not recognize its objective reality and its efficacy, we fall back into that form of idealism—called "economism" —which Marx so often denounced.[7]

Why are we dissatisfied? Why do we react against Guérin's brilliant, false demonstrations? Because Marxism ought to study real men in depth, not dissolve them

[7] As for that so-called Montagnard bourgeoisie made up of purchasers of national properties and army contractors, I believe it was invented for the needs of the argument. Guérin reconstructs the skeleton from a single bone, like Cuvier [the paleontologist]. This bone is the presence of the wealthy Cambon at the Convention. Cambon was indeed a Montagnard, in favor of war, and a purchaser of national properties. It was Cambon, in fact, who instigated the decree of December 15, of which Robespierre quite clearly disapproved. But he was influenced by Dumouriez. The purpose of the decree—at the end of a very long history in which this General and the army contractors play a part—was to permit the seizure and sale of ecclesiastical and aristocratic property which would allow the circulation of the French assignat in Belgium. The decree was passed *in spite of* the risk of war with England, but in itself and in the eyes of Cambon and all those who supported it, it bore no positive relation to the economic rivalry between France and England. The purchasers of national properties were monopolists and profoundly hostile to the price ceilings. They had no particular interest in pushing a war to the death, and in 1794 many among them would have been content with a compromise. The army contractors, suspect, under strict surveillance, sometimes arrested, did not constitute a social force. One must admit, willy-nilly, that between 1793 and 1794 the Revolution escaped from the control of the grands bourgeois only to fall into the hands of the petite bourgeoisie. The latter continued the war and, along with the populace, pushed the revolutionary movement against the grande bourgeoisie, later turning it against the populace; this was its own end and the end of the Revolution. If Robespierre and the Montagnards on December 15 were not more strongly opposed to the extension of the war, this was *primarily* for *political* reasons (the very opposite of Girondist reasons). Peace would have appeared as a triumph on the part of the Gironde; but the rejection of the decree of December 15 would have been the prelude to peace. Robespierre was afraid *at that time* that the peace would be only a temporary truce and that a second coalition would quickly arise.

in a bath of sulphuric acid. Now the rapid, schematic explanation of the war as an operation of *the* commercial bourgeoisie causes those men whom we know well to disappear—Brissot, Guadet, Gensonné, Vergniaud— or else it constitutes them, in the final analysis, as the purely passive instruments of their class. But at the end of 1791 the upper bourgeoisie was in the process of losing control of the Revolution (it recovered it only in 1794). The new men who were rising to power were petits bourgeois, more or less *déclassé*, poor, without too many connections, who had passionately bound up their own destiny with that of the Revolution. To be sure, they were subjected to certain influences; they were caught up by "high society" (the "best people" of Paris, very different from the good society of Bordeaux). But they were never able in any way to express spontaneously the collective reaction of the Bordeaux shipowners and commercial imperialism. They favored the development of wealth, but the idea of risking the Revolution in a war to assure a profit to certain circles of the grande bourgeoisie was completely alien to them. Moreover, Guérin's theory leads us to this surprising conclusion: the bourgeoisie, which derives its profit from foreign trade, throws France into a war against the Emperor of Austria in order to destroy the power of England; at the same time its delegates in power do everything to keep England out of the war. One year later, when war is finally declared against the British, this same bourgeoisie, discouraged *at the moment of success,* no longer has any desire for war at all; and it is the bourgeoisie of the new landed proprietors (who have no interest in prolonging the conflict) which has to take over the war.

Why this long discussion? To show by the example

of one of the best Marxist writers that if one totalizes
too quickly, if one transforms—without evidence—
signification into intention, and result into an objective
deliberately aimed at, then the real is lost. Also, that
we must at all cost guard against replacing real, perfectly defined groups (*la Gironde*) by insufficiently determined collectivities (*the bourgeoisie* of importers
and exporters). The Girondists existed, they pursued
definite ends, they made History within a precise situation and on the basis of external conditions. They believed they were juggling with the Revolution for their
own advantage; in fact, they made it more radical and
democratic. It is in terms of this *political* contradiction
that they must be understood and explained. Of course,
someone will tell us that the proclaimed goal of the
followers of Brissot is a mask, that these bourgeois revolutionaries considered themselves and presented themselves as illustrious Romans, that it is the objective result which really defines what they did. But we must
be careful: the original thought of Marx, as we find it in
*The Eighteenth Brumaire of Louis Napoleon Bona-
parte*, attempts a difficult synthesis of intention and of
result; the contemporary use of that thought is superficial and dishonest. If we push the Marxist metaphor to
its limit, in fact, we arrive at a new idea of human action. Imagine an actor who is playing Hamlet and who
is caught up in his role. He crosses his mother's room
to kill Polonius hidden behind the arras. But that is not
what he is actually doing. He crosses a stage before an
audience and passes from "court side" to "garden side"
in order to earn his living, to win fame, and this real
activity defines his position in society. But one cannot
deny that these *real* results are present in some way in
his imaginary act. One cannot deny that the movement

of the imaginary prince expresses in a certain indirect
and refracted manner the actor's real movement, nor
that the very way in which he *takes himself* for Hamlet
is his own way of *knowing himself* an actor. To return
to our Romans of 1789, their way of *calling* themselves
Cato is their way of *making* themselves bourgeois, members of a class which discovers History and which already wants to stop it, which claims to be universal
and which establishes the proud individualism of its
members upon a competitive economy—in short, the
heirs of a classical culture. Everything is there. It is one
and the same thing to declare oneself Roman and to
want to *stop* the Revolution. Or rather, the better one
can pose as Brutus or Cato, the better one will be able
to stop the Revolution. This thought, obscure even to
itself, sets up mystical ends which enclose the confused
awareness of its objective ends. Thus we may speak
simultaneously of a subjective drama (the simple play
of appearances which hides nothing, which contains no
"unconscious" element) and of an *objective, intentional*
organization of real means with a view to achieving real
ends—without any organization of all this by a consciousness or a premeditated will. Very simply, the
truth of the imaginary *praxis* is in the real *praxis,* and
the real, to the extent that it takes itself as merely
imaginary, includes implicit references to the imaginary *praxis* as to its interpretation. The bourgeois of
1789 does not pretend to be Cato in order to stop the
Revolution by denying History and by substituting
virtue for politics; neither does he tell himself that he
resembles Brutus in order to give himself a mythical
comprehension of an action which he carries out but
which escapes him. He does both at the same time.
And it is precisely this synthesis which allows us to dis-

cover an imaginary action in each one as a doublet and at the same time the matrix of real, objective action.

But if *that* is what is meant, then the followers of Brissot, at the very core of their ignorance, must be the responsible authors of the economic war. This external, stratified responsibility must have been internalized as a certain obscure awareness of their political drama. In short, it is men whom we judge and not physical forces. Now, in the name of that intransigent but strictly just conception which regulates the relation of subjective to objectification—a view with which I, for my part, am in complete agreement—we must acquit the Gironde on this count of the indictment; its dramas and its inward dreams do not refer to the future Anglo-French conflict any more than does the objective organization of its acts.

But very often today people reduce this difficult idea to a wretched truism. They willingly admit that Brissot did not know what he was doing, but they insist on the obvious fact that sooner or later the social and political structure of Europe had to become involved in a general war. Therefore, by declaring war on the Princes and on the Emperor, the Legislative Assembly declared it on the King of England. That is what it *was doing* without knowing it. Now this conception is by no means specifically Marxist; it limits itself to restating what everybody has always known: the consequences of our acts always end up by escaping us, since every concerted enterprise, as soon as it is realized, enters into relation with the entire universe, and since this infinite multiplicity of relations goes beyond our intention. If we look at things from this angle, human action is reduced to that of a physical force whose effect evidently depends upon the system in which it is exercised. But *for this very reason* one can no longer speak of *doing*. It is men who *do,* not avalanches. The bad faith of our Marxists consists in bringing two concepts into play at the same time so as to preserve the benefit of a teleological interpretation while concealing the abundant, highhanded use which they make of the explanation by finality. They employ the second concept to make it appear to everyone that there is a mechanistic interpretation of History—ends have disappeared. At the same time they make use of the first so as surreptitiously to transform into real objectives of a human activity the necessary but unforeseeable consequences which this activity entails. Hence that tedious vacillation in Marxist explanations. From one sentence to another the historical enterprise is defined implicitly *by goals* (which often are only unforeseen results) or reduced to the diffusion of a physical movement across an inert milieu. A contradiction? No. Bad faith. One must not confuse the scintillation of ideas with dialectic.

Marxist formalism is a project of elimination. The method is identical with Terror in its inflexible refusal to *differentiate;* its goal is total assimilation at the least possible effort. The aim is not to integrate what is different as such, while preserving for it a relative autonomy, but rather to suppress it. Thus the perpetual movement *toward identification* reflects the bureaucrats' practice of unifying everything. Specific determinations awaken in the theory the same suspicions as persons do in reality. For the majority of Marxists, to think is to claim to totalize and, under this pretext, to replace particularity by a universal. It is to claim to lead us back to the concrete and thereby present us with fundamental but abstract determinations. Hegel at least allowed the particular to continue to exist as a surpassed particularity; the Marxist would believe that he was wasting his time if, for example, he tried to understand the originality of a bourgeois thought. In his eyes the only thing which matters is to show that the thought is a mode of idealism. Naturally he will recognize that a book written in 1956 does not resemble a book of 1930; this is because the world has changed, and ideology, too, which reflects the world from the point of view of a particular class. The bourgeoisie enters into a period of withdrawal; idealism will then assume another form so as to express this new position, this new tactic. But for the intellectual Marxist, this dialectical movement does not leave the plane of universality; the problem is to define it in its generality and to show that in the work considered, it is expressed in the same way as in all others which appeared at the same date. The Marxist therefore is impelled to take as an appearance the real content of behavior or of a thought; when he dissolves the particular in the Universal, he has the satisfaction of believing that he is reducing appearance to truth. Actually, by defining his *subjective* concept of reality, he has only defined himself.

Marx was so far from this false universality that he attempted to generate his knowledge dialectically in man, rising progressively from the broadest determinations to the most precise. In a letter to Lassalle, he defines his method as a pursuit which "rises from the abstract to the concrete." And for him the concrete is the hierarchical totalization of determinations and of hierarchized realities. For "the population is an abstraction if I omit, for example, the classes from which it is formed; these classes in turn are a word empty of meaning if I ignore the factors on which they are based— for example, work for wages, capital, etc." But inversely these fundamental determinations would remain abstract if we were to sever them from the realities which support them and which they modify. The population of England in the middle of the nineteenth century is an abstract universal, "a chaotic representation of the aggregate," so long as it is considered as a simple quantity. But the economic categories are themselves insufficiently determined if we do not first establish that they are applied to the English population; that is, to real men who live and make History in the capitalist country whose industrialization is most advanced. It is in the name of this totalization that Marx will be able to show the action of superstructures on substructural facts.

But if it is true that "the population" is an abstract concept so long as we have not defined it by its most fundamental structures (that is, so long as it has not taken its place, as a concept, within the framework of the Marxist interpretation), it is also true that when this framework exists, and for the intellectual who is experienced in the dialectical method, men, their objectifications and their labors, human relations, are finally *what is the most concrete*. A first approximation painlessly puts them at their proper level and discovers their general determinations. Where we already know the direction and character of a society, the development of its productive forces, and its relations of production, there every new fact (a man, an action, a work) appears as *already situated* in its generality; progress consists in clarifying the more profound structures by means of the originality of the established fact in order to be able in turn to determine this originality by the fundamental structures. There is a double movement. But today's Marxists behave as if Marxism did not exist and as if each one of them, in every intellectual act, reinvented it, finding it each time exactly equal to itself. They behave as if the man or the group or the book appeared to them in the form of "a chaotic representation of the aggregate" (although they know very well that a particular book is by a certain bourgeois author in a certain bourgeois society at a certain moment of its development and that all these qualities have been already established by other Marxists). All this takes place for these theoreticians as if it were absolutely necessary to reduce this so-called abstraction—the political conduct of a particular individual or his literary work—to a "truly" concrete reality (capitalist imperialism, idealism), which *in fact* is only *in itself* an abstract determination. Thus the *concrete reality* of a philosophical work will be *idealism;* the work represents only a transient mode of it. In itself it is characterized only by deficiency and nothingness; what makes its *being* is its permanent reducibility to substance—"idealism." Thus a perpetual process of fetishizing.[8]

[8] Yet it is a Marxist, Henri Lefebvre, who in my opinion has provided a simple and faultless method for integrating sociology and history in the perspective of a materialist dialectic. The passage is worth quoting in its entirety. Lefebvre begins by pointing out that a living rural community appears first in *a horizontal complexity;* we are dealing with a human group in possession of techniques and with a definite agricultural productivity related to these techniques, along with the social structure which they determine and which conditions them in return. This human group, whose characteristics depend in large part upon great national and world-wide structures (which, for example, condition specializations on the national scale), offers a multiplicity of aspects which must be described and fixed (demographic aspects, family structure, habitat, religion, etc.). But Lefebvre hastens to add that this horizontal complexity has as its counterpart a "vertical" or "historical complexity": in the rural world we observe "the coexistence of formations of various ages and dates." The two complexities "react upon one another." He notes, for example, the very striking fact that history alone (not empirical, statistical sociology) can explain the rural American fact: the settlers came into free

Consider Lukacs. His expression, "the permanent carnival of fetishized interiority," is not only pedantic and vague; its very appearance is suspect. The addition of one violent and concrete word, "carnival," which suggests color, agitation, noise, is for the obvious purpose of covering up the poverty of the concept and its gratuity. For ultimately either the intention is merely to indicate the literary subjectivism of the period—and this is to state the obvious since the subjectivism was openly *proclaimed*—or else it is to claim that the relation of the author to his subjectivity was necessarily a process of fetishizing, and this is said much too quickly. Wilde, Proust, Bergson, Gide, Joyce—there are as many different relations to the subjective as there are names. *On the contrary*, one could show that neither Joyce nor

---

territory and occupied the land when cities were already long established (whereas the city in Europe developed in the midst of a rural setting). Here we will find the reason why rural culture is, strictly speaking, nonexistent in the U.S.A. or is at most a degraded urban culture.

In order to study such complexity (in cross section) and such a reciprocity of interrelations—without getting lost in it—Lefebvre proposes "a very simple method employing auxiliary techniques and comprising several phases:

"(a) *Descriptive*. Observation but with a scrutiny guided by experience and by a general theory. . . .

"(b) *Analytico-Regressive*. Analysis of reality. Attempt to *date* it precisely.

"(c) *Historical-Genetic*. Attempt to rediscover the present, but elucidated, understood, explained." (Henri Lefebvre: "Perspectives de sociologie rurale," *Cahiers de sociologie,* 1953.)

We have nothing to add to this passage, so clear and so rich, except that we believe that this method, with its phase of phenomenological description and its double movement of regression followed by progress, is valid—with the modifications which its objects may impose upon it—*in all the domains of anthropology.* Furthermore, it is this method which we shall apply, as we shall see later, to significations, to individuals themselves, and to the concrete relations among individuals. This method alone can be heuristic; it alone at once defines the originality of the fact and makes comparisons possible. We only regret that Lefebvre has not found imitators among the rest of Marxist intellectuals.

Proust nor Gide fetishizes interiority—not Joyce, who wanted to create a mirror of the world, to challenge the common language, and to lay down the foundations of a new linguistic universality; nor Proust, who dissolved the Self in his analyses and whose sole purpose was to use the magic of pure memory so that the *real, external* object might be reborn in its absolute uniqueness; nor Gide, who kept himself within the tradition of Aristotelian humanism. Lukacs's notion is not derived from experience; it has not been established by studying the conduct of particular men; its false individuality is a Hegelian idea (like the unhappy Consciousness or the Beautiful Soul), which creates for itself its own instruments.

This lazy Marxism puts everything into everything, makes real men into the symbols of its myths; thus the only philosophy which can really grasp the complexity of the human being is transformed into a paranoiac dream. "To situate," for Garaudy, means, on the one hand, to link together the universality of a period, of a condition, of a class, and its relations of force with other classes and, on the other hand, the universality of a defensive or offensive attitude (a social practice or an ideological concept). But this system of correspondences between abstract universals is constructed deliberately to suppress the group or the man whom one claims to consider. If I want to understand Valéry—that petit bourgeois intellectual, sprung from that historical, concrete group, the French petite bourgeoisie at the end of the last century—then it is better for me not to consult the Marxists. In place of that numerically defined group, they will substitute *the idea* of its material conditions, of its position with respect to other groups (the petit bourgeois is always viewed *"from the one* side

. . . from the other"), and of its internal contradictions. We shall go back to the economic category, we shall find petit bourgeois property threatened at the same time by capitalist concentration and by popular demands; here is naturally the basis for the fluctuations of its social attitude. All that is quite correct. This skeleton of universality is truth itself *at its abstract level.* Let us go further: when the questions proposed remain within the domain of the universal, these schematic elements by their combination sometimes enable us to find answers.

But the problem concerns Valéry. Our abstract Marxist is not moved in the slightest. He will affirm the constant progress of materialism; then he will describe a certain idealism—analytic, mathematical, slightly tinged with pessimism—which he will finally offer us as a simple riposte, already defensive, to the materialistic rationalism of the rising philosophy. All its characteristics will be determined dialectically in relation to this materialism; it is always the materialism which is presented as the independent variable, which never undergoes any modification. This "thought" of the subject of history, an expression of historical *praxis,* has the role of an *active* inductor; in the works and ideas of the bourgeoisie one doesn't want to see anything but *practical* attempts (and always vain ones) to parry more and more violent attacks, to fill the pockets, to stop up the breaches and the fissures, to assimilate hostile infiltrations. The almost total indetermination of ideology thus described will permit the making of an abstract scheme to preside over the composition of contemporary works. At that moment the analysis stops, and the Marxist judges his work finished. As for Valéry, he has disappeared.

For our part, we too hold that *the idealism is an object*. The proof is that we give a name to it, we teach it, we adopt it or fight against it; it has a history, and it does not cease to evolve. It was once a living philosophy, it is now a dead philosophy. It testified to a certain relation among men; today it manifests nonhuman relations (among bourgeois intellectuals, for example). But precisely for this reason, we refuse to make of it an a priori transparent to the mind; this does not mean that in our view this philosophy is a *thing*. No. We simply consider it to be a special type of reality—an idea-object. This reality belongs to the category of "collectives," which we shall attempt to examine a little later. For us, its existence is real, and we shall never apprehend anything of it except by means of experiment, observation, phenomenological description, understanding, and specialized works. This *real* object appears to us to be a determination of the objective culture; it was once the vigorous, critical thought of a rising class; it became for the middle classes a certain mode of conservative thought (there are others of these and, in particular, a certain scientistic materialism which, according to the occasion, seeks to legitimize utilitarianism or racism). This "collective apparatus," in our view, offers a totally different reality from, for example, a Gothic church, but it possesses, just as much as the church, actual *presence* and historical *depth*. Many Marxists claim to see in it only the common signification of thoughts scattered across the world; we are more realists than they are. Here is one more reason why we refuse to invert the terms, to make a fetish out of the apparatus and to take idealist intellectuals for its manifestations. We see Valéry's ideology as the concrete, unique product of an existent who is characterized *in part* by his *relations with* idealism but who must be interpreted in his particularity and first of all in terms of the concrete group from which he has sprung. This in no way means that his relations do not include those of his environment, of his class, etc., but only that we grasp them a posteriori by observation and in our attempt to totalize the sum of possible knowledge on this question. Valéry is a petit bourgeois intellectual, no doubt about it. But not every petit bourgeois intellectual is Valéry. The heuristic inadequacy of contemporary Marxism is contained in these two sentences. Marxism lacks any hierarchy of mediations which would permit it to grasp the process which produces the person and his product inside a class and within a given society at a given historical moment. Characterizing Valéry as a petit bourgeois and his work as idealist, the Marxist will find in both alike only what he has put there. It is because of this deficiency that he ends up getting rid of the particular by defining it as the simple effect of chance. Engels writes:

> That such a man, and precisely this man, arises at a determined period and in a given country is naturally pure chance. But, lacking Napoleon, another man would have filled his place. . . . The same is true of all chance events and of all that appears to be chance in history. The farther removed the province which we are exploring is from economy, and the more it cloaks itself in an abstract ideological character, the more chance we find in its development. . . . But trace the middle axis of the curve. . . . This axis tends to become parallel to that of the economic development.

In other words, the concrete character of *this* man is, for Engels, an "abstract ideological character." Only the middle axis of the curve (of a life, of a history, of a party, or of a social group) has anything real or intelligible, and this moment of universality corresponds to another universality (economics proper). Existentialism considers Engels's statement an arbitrary limitation of the dialectical movement, an arresting of thought, a refusal to understand. Existentialism refuses to abandon the real life to the unthinkable chances of birth for the sake of contemplating a universality limited to reflecting indefinitely upon itself.[9] It intends, without being unfaithful to Marxist principles, to find mediations which allow the individual concrete—the particular life, the real and dated conflict, the person—to emerge from the background of the *general* contradictions of productive forces and relations of production.

Contemporary Marxism shows, for example, that Flaubert's realism offers a kind of reciprocal symbolization in relation to the social and political evolution of the petite bourgeoisie of the Second Empire. But it *never* shows the genesis of this reciprocity of perspective. We do not know why Flaubert preferred literature to everything else, nor why he lived like an anchorite, nor why he wrote *these* books rather than those of Duranty or the Goncourt brothers. Marxism situates but no longer ever discovers anything. It allows other disciplines, without principles, to establish the exact circumstances of the life and of the person, and it arrives finally at demonstrating that its schemata have been once more verified. Things being what they are, the class struggle having assumed this or that form, Flaubert, who belonged to the bourgeoisie, had to live as he lived and to write as he wrote. What is passed over in silence

---

[9] These parallel middle axes are ultimately reduced to a single line: considered from this angle, relations of production, social-political structures, and ideologies seem to be (as in Spinoza's philosophy) merely "various translations of the same sentence."

is the signification of these four words, "belonged to the bourgeoisie." For it is neither his rental income nor the strictly intellectual nature of his work which first makes Flaubert a bourgeois. He *belongs* to the bourgeoisie because he was born in it; that is, because he appeared in the midst of a family *already bourgeois*,[1] the head of which, a surgeon at Rouen, was carried along by the ascending movement of his class. If Flaubert reasons and feels as a bourgeois, this is because he has been made such at a period when he could not even comprehend the meaning of the gestures and the roles which were imposed upon him. Like all families, this family was particular. The mother was related to the nobility, the father was the son of a village veterinarian; Gustave's older brother, superficially more gifted, became very early the object of Gustave's hatred. It is, then, inside the particularity of a history, through the peculiar contradictions of *this* family, that Gustave Flaubert unwittingly served his class apprenticeship. Chance does not exist or, at least, not in the way that is generally believed. The child becomes this or that because he lives the universal as particular. This child lived, *in the particular*, the conflict between the religious ceremonies of a monarchist regime which was claiming a renascence and the irreligion of his father, a petit bourgeois intellectual and son of the French Revolution.

Considered in general terms, this conflict expressed the struggle of the former landowners against the purchasers of national property and the industrial bourgeoisie. This contradiction (masked, however, under the

---

[1] It is also possible to *come into* the bourgeoisie. But a person who becomes a petit bourgeois after crossing a boundary line will never be the same petit bourgeois that he would have been if he had been one by birth.

Restoration, by a temporary equilibrium) Flaubert lived for himself alone and by himself. His aspirations toward nobility and especially toward faith were continually beaten down by the analytical mind of his father. Consequently there was set up *inside him* this overwhelming father who did not cease, even after death, to destroy God, his principal adversary, nor to reduce the impulses of his son to bodily humors. The small Flaubert, however, lived all this through in darkness—that is, without gaining any real awareness, but in panic, flight, bewilderment, and within the limits of his material circumstances as a bourgeois child, well nourished, well cared for, but helpless and separated from the world. It was *as a child* that he lived his future condition through the professions which would be offered to him. His hatred of his older brother, a brilliant student at the Faculté de Médecine, barred the path to the Sciences; that is, Gustave neither wished nor dared to become a part of the "petit bourgeois" elite. There remained the Law. Through these professions, which he regarded as inferior, he had a horror of his own class; and this very horror was at once an attainment of awareness and a definitive alienation from the petite bourgeoisie. He lived also the bourgeois death, that solitude which accompanies us from the moment of birth, but he lived it by means of the family structures: the garden where he played with his sister was next to the laboratory in which his father practiced dissection; death, corpses, his young sister who was soon to die, his father's science and irreligion—all had to be unified in a complex and very particular attitude. The explosive mixture of naïve scientism and religion without God which constituted Flaubert, and which he tried to overcome by his love of formal art, can be explained if we understand that everything took

place *in childhood;* that is, in a condition radically distinct from the adult condition. It is childhood which
sets up unsurpassable prejudices, it is childhood which,
in the violence of training and the frenzy of the tamed
beast, makes us experience the fact of our belonging to
our environment *as a unique event.*

Today psychoanalysis alone enables us to study the
process by which a child, groping in the dark, is going
to attempt to play, without understanding it, the social
role which adults impose upon him.[2] Only psychoanalysis will show us whether he stifles in his role, whether he
seeks to escape it, or is entirely assimilated into it. Psychoanalysis alone allows us to discover the whole man
in the adult; that is, not only his present determinations
but also the weight of his history. And one would be
entirely wrong in supposing that this discipline is opposed to dialectical materialism. To be sure, amateurs
in the West have constructed "analytical" theories of
society or of History which indeed end up in idealism.
How many times has someone attempted the feat of
psychoanalyzing Robespierre for us without even understanding that the contradictions in his behavior
were conditioned by the objective contradictions of the
situation. When one has understood how the bourgeoisie of *Thermidor,*[3] paralyzed by the democratic regime, found itself forced by practical necessity to demand a military dictatorship, then it is most annoying
to read from the pen of a psychiatrist that Napoleon is

[2] When Sartre speaks of psychoanalysis, he is not referring to traditional Freudianism with its dependence on the concept of the unconscious and universal symbolism. In *Being and Nothingness* he has
presented the fundamental principles for an existential psychoanalysis,
indebted to Freud but consistent with Sartre's own existentialism as
a philosophy of freedom. H.B.
[3] The eleventh month (July–August) of the calendar adopted during the French Revolution. H.B.

explained by his "will to fail." De Man, the Belgian socialist, went still further when he tried to explain class conflicts by "the Proletariat's inferiority complex." Inversely, Marxism, once it became a universal Knowledge, wanted to integrate psychoanalysis into itself by first twisting its neck. Marxism made of it a dead idea which quite naturally found its place in a desiccated system; it was idealism returning in disguise, an avatar of the fetishism of interiority. In the one case as in the other a method has been transformed into dogmatism: the philosophers of psychoanalysis find their justification in the Marxist "schematizers" and vice versa. The fact is that dialectical materialism cannot deprive itself much longer of the one privileged mediation which permits it to pass from general and abstract determinations to particular traits of the single individual. Psychoanalysis has no principles, it has no theoretical foundation; and this is quite all right if it accompanies—as in the work of Jung and in certain works of Freud—a completely innocuous mythology. In fact, it is a method which is primarily concerned with establishing the way in which the child lives his family relations inside a given society. And this does not mean that it raises any doubts as to the priority of institutions. Quite the contrary, its object itself depends on the structure of a *particular* family, and this is only a certain individual manifestation of the family structure appropriate to such and such a class under such and such conditions. Thus psychoanalytic monographs—if it were always possible to have them—would by themselves throw light upon the evolution of the French family between the eighteenth and the twentieth century, which in its turn would express in its own way the general evolution of the relations of production.

Today's Marxists are concerned only with adults; reading them, one would believe that we are born at the age when we earn our first wages. They have forgotten their own childhoods. As we read them, everything seems to happen as if men experienced their alienation and their reification *first in their own work,* whereas in actuality each one lives it *first,* as a child, *in his parents' work.* Dead set against interpretations too exclusively sexual, Marxists make use of them in order to condemn a method of interpretation which claims only to put History in place of nature in each person. They have not yet understood that sexuality is only one way of living the totality of our condition—at a certain level and within the perspective of a certain individual venture. Existentialism, on the contrary, believes that it can integrate the psychoanalytic method which discovers the point of insertion for man and his class—that is, the particular family—as a mediation between the universal class and the individual. The family in fact is constituted by and in the general movement of History, but is experienced, on the other hand, as an absolute in the depth and opaqueness of childhood.

The Flaubert family was of the semi-domestic type; it was a little behind the industrial families which the father Flaubert cared for or visited. The father Flaubert, who felt that he was "wronged" by his "patron" Dupuytren, terrorized everyone with his own worth and ability, his Voltairian irony, his terrible angers and fits of melancholy. We will also easily understand that the bond between the small Gustave and his mother was never determining; she was only a reflection of the terrible doctor. Thus we have before us an almost tangible cleavage which will often separate Flaubert from his contemporaries; in a century when the conjugal family is the type current among the wealthy bourgeoisie, when Du Camp and Le Poittevin represent children freed from the *patria potestas*, Flaubert is characterized by a "fixation" on his father. Baudelaire, on the other hand, born the same year, will be fixed all his life on his mother. And this difference is explained by the difference in their respective environments. Flaubert's bourgeoisie is harsh, new. (His mother, vaguely connected with the nobility, represents a class of landowners in process of liquidation; the father comes straight out of a village and wears strange, peasant clothing even at Rouen—a goatskin in winter.) This bourgeoisie comes from the country; and it returns there, too, since it uses its gradually won wealth to buy land. Baudelaire's family, bourgeois, urban for many years already, considers itself in some small way belonging to the new nobility (*la noblesse de robe*); it owns stocks and bonds. Sometimes, between two masters, the mother appeared all alone in the glory of her independence. Later it was all in vain for Aupick to play at being the "boss"; Mme Aupick, stupid and rather vain, but charming and favored by her period, never ceased to exist *in her own right*.

But we must be careful. Each one lives his first years, distracted or bewildered, as a profound and solitary reality. Here the internalization of the external is an irreducible fact. The "flaw" of the small Baudelaire is, to be sure, the widowhood and remarriage of a very pretty mother; but it is also a peculiar quality of his own life, a disequilibrium, an unhappiness which will pursue him until his death. Flaubert's "fixation" on his father is the expression of a group structure, and it is his hatred of the bourgeois, his "hysterical" crises, his monastic vocation. Psychoanalysis, working within a dialectical totalization, refers on the one side to objective structures, to material conditions, and on the other to the action upon our adult life of the childhood we never wholly surpass. Henceforth it becomes impossible to connect *Madame Bovary* directly to the political-social structure and to the evolution of the petite bourgeoisie; the book will have to be referred back to contemporary reality insofar as it was lived by Flaubert through his childhood. There results from this a certain discrepancy, to be sure; there is a sort of hysteresis on the part of the work in relation to the very period in which it appears; this is because it must unite within itself a number of contemporary significations and certain others which express a state recent but already surpassed by society. This *hysteresis*, always neglected by the Marxists, accounts in turn for the veritable social reality in which *contemporary* events, products, and acts are characterized by the extraordinary diversity of their temporal depth. There will come a moment at which Flaubert will appear to be *in advance* of his period (at the time of *Madame Bovary*) because he is *behind it*, because his book, in disguised form, expresses to a generation disgusted with romanticism the post-romantic despairs of a student of 1830. The objective meaning of the book —which the Marxists, as good disciples of Taine, take simply as conditioned by the moment represented in the author—is the result of a compromise between what this new generation of readers claims in terms of its own history and what the author can offer to it from his own; that is, it realizes the paradoxical union of two past moments of this intellectual petite bourgeoisie (1830 and 1845). It is in these terms that one will be able to *use* the book in a new perspective as a weapon against a class or a government.[4] But Marxism has nothing to fear from these new methods; they simply reinstate concrete regions of the real, and the individual person's distress takes on its true meaning when one recalls that it expresses concretely the alienation of man. Existentialism, aided by psychoanalysis, can study today only situations in which man has been lost since childhood, for there are no others in a society founded on exploitation.[5]

[4] These young readers are *defeatists:* they demand that their writers show that action is impossible in order to blot out their shame at having failed in their attempt at Revolution. For them realism is the condemnation of reality: life is absolute disaster. Flaubert's *pessimism* has its positive counterpart (aesthetic mysticism), which is found everywhere in *Madame Bovary,* which stares us in the face but which the public did not "take in" because it wasn't looking for it. Baudelaire alone saw it clearly. *"The Temptation* and *Madame Bovary* have the same subject," he wrote. But what could he accomplish against that *new collective event* which is the transformation of a book by reading? This meaning of *Madame Bovary* still remains veiled today; every young man who becomes acquainted with this work today, unwittingly discovers it across the dead who have changed its direction.

[5] Nevertheless, one question arises: Marxists hold that the social conduct of an individual is conditioned by the general conditions of his class. By the dialectical movement, these interests—at first abstract—become concrete forces which fetter us. It is these which limit our horizon; it is these which are expressed by our own mouth and which hold us back when we would like to understand our acts through and through, when we try to wrench ourselves out of our milieu. Is this thesis incompatible with the idea of a conditioning of our present conduct by our childhood? I do not believe so. It is easy to see, on the contrary, that the analytical mediation does not change anything. Of course, our prejudices, our ideas, our beliefs, are for the majority of us unsurpassable *because they have been experienced first in childhood;* it is our childish blindness, our prolonged panic which accounts—in part—for our irrational reactions, for our resistance to reason. But precisely what was this unsurpassable childhood, if not a particular way of living the general interests of our surroundings? Nothing is changed; on the contrary, tenacity, mad and criminal passion, even heroism, all recover their *true density,* their roots, their past. Psychoanalysis, conceived as a mediation, does not bring to bear any new principle of explanation. It is careful not to deny the direct,

We have not finished with *mediations*. At the level of
the relations of production and at that of political-social
structures, the unique person is found conditioned by
his *human relations*. No doubt this conditioning, in its
first, general truth, refers to "the conflict of productive
forces with the relations of production." But all this is
not *lived* so simply. Or rather the question is to know
whether *reduction* is possible. The person lives and
knows his condition more or less clearly through the
groups he belongs to. The majority of these groups are
local, definite, immediately given. It is clear, in fact,
that the factory worker is subject to the pressure of his
"production group," but if, as is the case at Paris, he
lives rather far from his place of work, he is equally subject to the pressure of his "residential group." Now
these groups exert various actions upon their members;
sometimes, even, the particular "block," the "housing
project," the "neighborhood," checks in each person the
impetus given by the factory or the shop. The problem
is to know whether Marxism will dissolve the residential
group into its elements or whether it will recognize in it
a relative autonomy and a power of mediation. The decision is not so easy. On one side, in fact, one easily sees
that the "lag" between the residential group and the
production group, along with the "retardation" which
the former exerts on the latter, only helps to verify the
fundamental analyses of Marxism. In one sense there is
nothing new here; and the Communist Party itself has
shown since its birth that it is aware of this contradiction; wherever possible it organizes cells based on
working locations rather than residential districts. On

present relation of the individual to his environment or to his class; it
reintroduces historicity and negativity in the very way in which the
person realizes himself as a member of a well-defined social stratum.

the other side, it is everywhere apparent that the employer, when he attempts to "modernize" his methods, favors the constitution of extra-political groups as a check, the effect of which in France is certainly to remove the young from union and political activity.

At Annecy, for example, which is being industrialized very rapidly and which pushes tourists and vacationers over to those sections which border on the lake, researchers report that there is a proliferation of small groups (culture societies, sports groups, amateur radio clubs, etc.) whose character is very ambiguous. There is no doubt that they raise the cultural level of their members—which in any event will remain an acquisition of the proletariat—but it is certain that they are obstacles to emancipation. Furthermore, it would be necessary to consider whether in these societies (which in many cases the employers have shrewdly left completely autonomous) culture is not *necessarily* oriented (that is, in the direction of bourgeois ideology; statistics show that the books most often requested by workers are the bourgeois best-sellers). These considerations tend to make of the "relation to the group" a reality that is lived for itself and which possesses a particular efficacy. In the case which concerns us, for example, there is no doubt that it is interposed as a screen between the individual and the general interests of his class. This group consistency (which must not be confused with any sort of collective consciousness) would by itself justify what the Americans call "micro-sociology." Even more, sociology in the United States is developed because of its very efficiency. To those who may be tempted to see in sociology only a mode of idealist, static knowing, the sole function of which is to conceal history, I would recall the fact that in the United States it is the employer who favors this discipline and who in particular sponsors the research which studies restricted groups as the totalization of human contacts in a defined situation. Moreover, American neo-paternalism and *Human Engineering* are based almost exclusively on the work of sociologists. But one must not make those factors an excuse for adopting immediately the reverse attitude and summarily rejecting sociology on the ground that it is "a class weapon in the hands of the capitalists." If it is an effective weapon—and it has proved that it is one—this is because it contains some truth; and if it is "in the hands of the capitalists," this is one more reason for snatching it away from the capitalists and turning it back against them.

No doubt the principle of sociological research is often a disguised idealism. In the work of Lewin, for example (as with all Gestaltists), there is a fetishism of totalization; instead of seeing in it the real movement of History, Lewin hypostasizes it and *realizes* it in *already made* totalities. He writes: "It is necessary to consider the situation, with all its social and cultural implications, *as a dynamic, concrete whole.*" Or again: "The structural properties of a dynamic totality are not the same as those of its parts." On the one hand, we are presented with a synthesis of externality, and to this given totality the sociologist himself remains external. He wants to hold on to the benefits of teleology while at the same time maintaining the attitude of *positivism*— that is, while suppressing or disguising the ends of human activity. At this point sociology is posited for itself and is opposed to Marxism, not by affirming the provisional autonomy of its method—which would, on the contrary, provide the means for integrating it—but by affirming the radical autonomy of its object. First, it is an *ontological autonomy*. No matter what precaution one takes, one cannot prevent the group, thus conceived, from being a substantial unity—*even* and *especially* if, out of a desire for empiricism, one defines its existence by its simple function. Second, it is a *methodological autonomy*. In place of the movement of dialectical totalization, one substitutes actual totalities. This step naturally implies a refusal of dialectic and of history exactly because dialectic is at the start only the real movement of a unity in process of being made and not the study, not even the "functional" and "dynamic" study, of a unity already made. For Lewin, every law is a structural law and expresses a function or a functional relation between the parts of a whole. Precisely for this reason, he deliberately confines himself to the study of what Lefebvre called "horizontal complexity." He studies neither the history of the individual (psychoanalysis) nor that of the group. Lewin is the most open to Lefebvre's criticism, which we quoted earlier. His method claims to establish the functional characteristics of a rural community in the United States; but it will interpret all of them in relation to the variations of the totality. For this very reason, therefore, his method will be lacking in any history since it prohibits itself, for example, from explaining the remarkable religious homogeneity of a group of Protestant farmers. It is of little importance to Lewin to know that the total susceptibility of rural communities to urban models arises in the United States from the fact that the country was formed with the existing city in mind, by men who were already in possession of relatively advanced industrial techniques. Lewin would consider this explanation—to use his terminology—an Aristotelian causalism. But this means precisely that he is incapable of understanding the synthesis in the form of a dialectic; for him it would have to be *given*. Finally, it is a *reciprocal autonomy* of the experimenter and of the experimental group. The sociologist is not situated; or if he is, concrete precautions will suffice to desituate him. It may be that he tries to integrate himself into the group, but this integration is temporary; he knows that he will disengage himself, that he will record his observations objectively. In short, he resembles those detectives whom the movies often present to us as models, who win the confidence of a gang so as to be better able to trap it. Even if the sociologist and the detective participate in a collective action, it is evident that they put their act between parentheses, that they make these gestures for the benefit of a "higher interest."

We could make the same objections to the notion of "basic personality" which Kardiner attempts to introduce into American neo-culturalism. If we try to see in this only a certain way in which the person totalizes society in and by himself, the notion is useless, as we shall soon discover. It would be absurd and futile to speak, for example, of the "basic personality" of the French Proletarian if we have at our disposal a method enabling us to understand how the worker projects himself toward his own self-objectification in terms of material, historical conditions. If, on the contrary, we consider this personality to be an objective reality imposing itself on the members of the group, even if in the form of "their basic personality," this is a fetish. We posit man before man, and we re-establish the bond of causation. Kardiner situates his basic personality "halfway between the primary institutions (which express the action of the environment upon the individual) and the secondary institutions (which express the individual's reaction upon the environment)." In spite of everything, "circularity" remains static; moreover, nothing demonstrates better than this "halfway" position the uselessness of the notion proposed. It is true that the individual is conditioned by the social environment and that he turns back upon it to condition it in turn; it is this—and nothing else—which makes his reality. But if we can determine the primary institutions and follow the movement by which the individual makes himself by surpassing them, why do we need to put on these ready-made clothes along the way? The "basic personality" fluctuates between abstract universality a posteriori and concrete substance as a completely *made totality*. If we take it as some sort of *whole, pre-existing* the person about to be born, then either it stops History and reduces it to a discontinuity of types and styles of life, or it is itself going to be shattered by the continuous movement of History.

This sociological attitude is in its turn explained *historically*. Hyper-empiricism—which on principle neglects connections with the past—could arise only in a country whose History is relatively short. The wish to put the sociologist out of the experimental field expresses simultaneously a bourgeois "objectivism" and the sociologist's own experience of being excluded. Lewin, exiled from Germany and persecuted by the Nazis, improvises himself as a sociologist in order to find practical means to restore the German community which he considers destroyed by Hitler. But *for him*, exiled, powerless, and against a great part of the Germans, this restoration can be obtained only by external methods, by an action exerted with the co-operation of the Allies. It is this closed-off, distant Germany which, by excluding him, furnishes him with the theme of the dynamic totality. (In order to make Germany democratic, it would be necessary, he said, to give her other leaders, but these leaders would be obeyed only if the entire group were modified in such a way as to accept them.) It is noteworthy that this uprooted bourgeois does not take into consideration either the real contradictions which brought on Nazism or a class struggle which he has ceased to live on his own account. The cleavages in a society, its internal divisions —these are what a German worker could live in Germany, and these factors could give him an entirely different idea of the real conditions of de-Nazification. The sociologist, in fact, is an object of history; the sociology of "primitive peoples" is established on the basis of a more profound relation which may be, for example, colonialism. Research is a living relation between men (it is this same relation in its totality which Leiris has tried to describe in his admirable book *L'Afrique fantôme*). Indeed, the sociologist and his "object" form a couple, each one of which is to be interpreted by the other; the *relationship* between them must be itself interpreted as a moment of history.

If we take these precautions—that is, if we reintegrate the sociological moment into the historical totalization—is there, despite all, a relative independence for sociology? For our part, we do not doubt it. While Kardiner's theories are open to criticism, some of his reported research is of undeniable interest, in particular the study he has made of the Marquesas Islands. He points up a latent anxiety in the Islands' inhabitants, the origin of which is found in certain objective conditions—the threat of famine and the scarcity of women (100 women to 250 men). He derives both embalming and cannibalism from famine, as two contradictory reactions which are conditioned by their mutual opposition. He shows that homosexuality is the result of the scarcity of women (and of polyandry), but he goes further and is able to demonstrate, as the result of his investigation, that homosexuality is not simply a satisfaction of the sexual need but a form of revenge against the woman. Finally, the result of this state of affairs is a genuine indifference in the woman and a great gentleness on the part of the father in his relations with the children (the child grows up in the midst of *his* fathers) —hence the free development of the children and their precociousness. Precocity, homosexuality as a revenge against the woman who is hard and without tenderness, a latent anxiety expressing itself in various behavior patterns: those are irreducible notions, since they refer us to what has had to be *lived*. It matters little that Kardiner employs psychoanalytical concepts to describe them; the fact is that sociology can *establish* these characteristics as real relations among men. Kardiner's research does not contradict dialectical materialism, even if Kardiner's *ideas* remain opposed to it. We can learn in his study how the material fact of the scarcity of women is lived as a certain aspect of the relations between the sexes and of the males with each other. We are guided to a certain level of the concrete which contemporary Marxism systematically neglects.

American sociologists conclude from such reports that "the economic is not entirely determining." But this sentence is neither true nor false, since dialectic is not a determinism. If it is true that the Eskimos are "individualists" and the Dakotas co-operative, and true too that they resemble each other in "the way in which they produce their life," we should not conclude from this that there is a definitive insufficiency in the Marx-

ist method but merely that it has been insufficiently developed. This means that sociology in its investigation of
defined groups achieves, *because of* its empiricism,
known information which is capable of developing the
dialectical method by compelling it to push its totalization to include this information. The Eskimos' "individualism," if it exists, must be conditioned by factors of
the same order as those which were studied in the Mar-
quesan communities. In itself it is a fact (or, to use
Kardiner's term, a "style of life") which has nothing to
do with "subjectivity" and which is disclosed in the behavior of individuals within the group and in relation to
the daily realities of life (habitat, meals, festivals, etc.)
and even of work. But, to the extent that sociology is
by itself a *prospective attention* directing itself on this
kind of facts, it is a heuristic method and it compels
Marxism to become one. It reveals, indeed, new relations and it demands that they be attached to new conditions. The "scarcity of women," for example, is a
genuine material condition; it is economic *at least* to the
extent that economy is defined by scarcity; it is a quantitative relation which strictly conditions a need. But in
addition, Kardiner forgets what Levi Strauss has so well
demonstrated in his book *Les Structures élémentaires
de la parenté;* that is, that marriage is a form of total
commitment. A woman is not only a companion for the
bed; she is a worker, a productive force. "At the most
primitive levels where the harsh geographical environment and the rudimentary state of techniques make gar-
dening and hunting, the gathering and picking of food
equally hazardous, existence would be almost impossible for an individual abandoned to himself. . . . It is
no exaggeration to say that for such societies marriage
holds a vital importance for each individual . . . inter-

ested (first) in finding . . . a mate but also in prevent-
ing the occurrence among his group of those two ca-
lamities of primitive society: celibacy and orphanhood"
(pp. 48–9).

This means that we must never yield to simplifica-
tions based wholly on techniques or consider social conditions to be conditioned by techniques and tools in a
context peculiar to themselves alone. Aside from the
fact that traditions and history (Lefebvre's vertical
complexity) intervene at the same level as work and
needs, there exist other material conditions (the scarcity of women is one of them) which reciprocally condition techniques and the real level of life. Thus the
numerical relation between the sexes assumes more importance for production and for suprastructural relations when famine is more of a threat and instruments
more rudimentary. The point is to subordinate nothing a
priori. It would be to no purpose to say that the scarcity
of women is a simple natural fact (contrasting it with
the institutional character of techniques), since this
scarcity never appears except inside a community. On
these terms nobody can any longer criticize the Marxist interpretation as being incompletely "determining";
it is sufficient in fact that the regressive-progressive
method take into account *at the same time* the circularity of the material conditions and the mutual conditioning of the human relations established on that basis.
(The immediately real connection, *on its own level,*
bringing together the hardness of the women, the indul-
gence of the fathers, the resentment which results in
homosexual tendencies, and the precocity of the children, is founded on polyandry, which is—on its own
ground—itself a group's reaction to scarcity. But these
various characteristics are not already contained *in* the

polyandry like eggs in a basket; by their reciprocal action, they are enriched as a *way of living* the polyandry by perpetually going beyond it.) In this prospective form, with its absence of theoretical foundation and the precision of its auxiliary method—research, tests, statistics, etc.—sociology, a temporary moment of the historical totalization, discovers new mediations between concrete men and the material conditions of their life, between human relations and the relations of production, between persons and classes (or some totally different sort of grouping).

We willingly grant that the *group* never has and never can have the type of metaphysical existence which people try to give to it. We repeat with Marxism: there are only men and real relations between men. From this point of view, the group is in one sense only a multiplicity of relations and of relations among those relations. And this certitude derives precisely from what we consider the reciprocal relation between the sociologist and his object; the researcher can be "outside" a group only to the degree that he is "inside" another group—except in limited cases in which this exile is the reverse side of a real act of exclusion. These diverse perspectives demonstrate to the inquirer that the community as such escapes him on all sides.

Yet this must not allow him to dispense with determining the type of reality and efficacy appropriate to the collective objects which people our social field and which may be conveniently called the intermundane.[6] An anglers' club is neither a small stone nor a supraconsciousness nor a simple verbal rubric to indicate concrete, particular relations among its members. It has

[6] The French word *intermonde* refers explicitly to the Epicurean concept of space between the worlds. H.B.

its bylaws, its officers, its budget, its procedure for re-
cruiting, its function; it is upon these terms that its
members have set up among themselves a certain type
of reciprocal relation. When we say there are only men
and real relations between men (for Merleau-Ponty I
add things also, and animals, etc.), we mean only that
we must expect to find the support of collective objects
in the concrete activity of individuals. We do not intend to *deny* the reality of these objects, but we claim
that it is *parasitical*.

Marxism is not far removed from our conception. But
in its present state, we may, from this point of view,
make two essential criticisms. To be sure, it shows how
"class interests" impose upon the individual against his
individual interests or how the market, at first a simple
complex of human relations, tends to become more real
than the sellers and their customers; but Marxism remains uncertain as to the nature and origin of these
"collectives." The theory of fetishism, outlined by Marx,
has never been developed; furthermore, it could not be
extended to cover all social realities. Thus Marxism,
while rejecting organicism, lacks weapons against it.
Marxism considers the market a *thing* and holds that its
inexorable laws contribute to reifying the relations
among men. But when suddenly—to use Henri Lefebvre's terms—a dialectical conjuring trick shows us
this monstrous abstraction as the veritable concrete
(we are speaking, naturally, of an alienated society)
while individuals (e.g., the worker submitted to Lassalle's law of wages) fall into abstraction, then we believe that we are returned to Hegelian idealism. For the
dependence of the worker who comes to sell his working
strength cannot under any circumstance signify that
this worker has fallen into an abstract existence. Quite

the contrary, the reality of the market, no matter how inexorable its laws may be, and even in its concrete appearance, rests on the reality of alienated individuals and on their separation. It is necessary to take up the study of collectives again from the beginning and to demonstrate that these objects, far from being characterized by the direct unity of a *consensus,* represent perspectives of flight. This is because, upon the basis of given conditions, the direct relations between persons depend upon other particular relations, and these on still others, and so on in succession, because there is an objective constraint in concrete relations. It is not the presence of others but their absence which establishes this constraint; it is not their union but their separation. For us the reality of the collective object rests on *recurrence.*[7] It demonstrates that the totalization is never achieved and that the totality exists at best only in the form of a *detotalized totality.*[8] As such these collectives exist. They are revealed immediately in action and in perception. In each one of them we shall always find a concrete materiality (a movement, the head office, a building, a word, etc.) which supports and manifests a flight which eats it away. I need only open my window: I see a church, a bank, a café—three collectives. This thousand-franc bill is another; still another is the newspaper I have just bought.

The second criticism which can be leveled against Marxism is the fact that it has never been concerned to study these objects for themselves; that is, on all levels of the social life. Now it is in terms of his relation with

[7] Sartre appears to be using the word *récurrence* in its philosophical sense, referring to the fact that one may extend to the whole of a series the property which can be ascribed to each of its terms. H.B.

[8] I have developed these comments in the second part of this work, *Critique of Dialectical Reason.*

collectives—that is, in his "social field" considered in its most immediate aspect—that man learns to know his condition. Here again the particular connections are one mode of realizing and of living the universal in its materiality. Here again this particularity has its peculiar opaqueness which does not allow us to dissolve it in fundamental determinations. This means that the "milieu" of our life, with its institutions, its monuments, its instruments, its cultural "infinites" (real like the Idea of Nature, or imaginary like Julien Sorel or Don Juan), its fetishes, its social temporality and its "hodological" space [9]—this *also* must be made the object of our study. These various realities, whose being is directly proportional to the non-being of humanity, sustain among themselves, through the intermediary of human relations, *and with us* a multiplicity of relations which can and must be studied in themselves. A product of his product, fashioned by his work and by the social conditions of production, man *at the same time* exists in the milieu of his products and furnishes the substance of the "collectives" which consume him. At each phase of life a short circuit is set up, a horizontal experience which contributes to change him upon the basis of the material conditions from which he has sprung. The child *experiences more than* just his family. He lives also—in part through the family—the collective landscape which surrounds him. It is again the generality of his class which is revealed to him in this individual experience.[1]

[9] Sartre has borrowed this expression from Lewin. "Hodological space" is the environment viewed in terms of our personal orientation. It sets up demands upon us and offers, as it were, pathways and obstacles to the fulfillments of our needs and desires. H.B.

[1] "Charlie Chaplin's whole life is contained in this landscape of brick and iron. . . . Lambeth Road is already the stage setting for *Easy Street* (*la rue des Bons Enfants*), where Charlie Chaplin pulls the gas lamp down over the head of the big Bully. Here are all the

The aim then is to construct horizontal syntheses in which the objects considered will develop freely their own structures and their laws. In relation to the vertical synthesis, this transversal totalization affirms both its dependence and its relative autonomy. By itself it is neither sufficient nor inconsistent. It is no use to try to throw "collectives" over to the side of pure appearance. Of course, we must not judge them by the awareness which contemporaries have of them, but we would lose their originality if we looked at them only from the point of view of their ultimate meanings. A person wishing to to study one of those culture groups which we find in certain factories, will not be quit of them by resorting to the old remark—the workers *believe that they are reading* (therefore the collective object is cultural), but in actuality they are only retarding their own attainment of self-awareness and delaying the emancipation of the Proletariat. For *it is very true* that they are delaying the moment of their new awareness, but *it is very true* also that they read and that their reading is effected at the center of a community which favors it and which is developed by means of it.

To use only one object, as an example, everyone will agree that a *city* is a material and social organization which derives its reality from the ubiquity of its absence. It is present in each one of its streets *insofar as* it is always elsewhere, and the myth of the capital with its *mysteries* demonstrates well that the opaqueness of direct human relations comes from this fact, that they are always conditioned by all others. *The Mysteries of Paris*

---

houses of his childhood, which Charlie Chaplin recalls, he says, with more emotion than the people." (Paul Gilson.) The collective environment of his wretched childhood becomes in him a sign, a myth, and a source of his creativity.

stem from the absolute interdependence of spots connected by their radical compartmentalization. Each urban collective has its own physiognomy. Some Marxists have drawn up felicitous classifications. Even from the point of view of economic evolution, they have distinguished agricultural cities from industrial cities, colonial cities, socialist cities, etc. They have shown for each type how the form and the division of labor, at the same time as the relations of production, would engender an organization and a particular distribution of urban functions. But that is not enough to let them catch up with experience. Paris and Rome differ profoundly from each other: Paris is a typically bourgeois city of the nineteenth century; Rome, at once both behind and ahead of the other city, is characterized by a center of aristocratic structure (poor and rich live on the same property, as in our capital before 1830), surrounded by modern sections which are inspired by American urbanism. It does not suffice to show that these structural differences correspond to fundamental differences in the economic development of the two countries and that Marxism, equipped as it is today, can account for them.[2] It is necessary to see also that the *constitutions* of these two cities immediately condition the concrete relations of their inhabitants. In the promiscuity of wealth and poverty, the Romans live in epitome the evolution of their national economy, but this promiscuity is *by itself* an immediate given of the social life. It manifests itself through human relations of a particular type; it presupposes that each one is rooted in the urban past, that there is a concrete bond between men and the ruins (which depends much less than one might believe on

[2] Rome is an agricultural center which has become an administrative capital. Industry, strictly speaking, has been little developed there.

the kind of work or class, since, after all, these ruins are inhabited and utilized by all—even more, perhaps, by the people than by the upper bourgeois), a certain organization of space—that is, roads which lead men toward other men or toward work. If we do not have the instruments necessary for studying the structure and the influence of this "social field," it will be altogether impossible for us, by simply determining the relations of production, to bring to light typically Roman attitudes. Some expensive restaurants are found in the poorest quarters. During the summer months the wealthy dine on café sidewalks. This fact—inconceivable in Paris—does not concern individuals only; by itself it speaks volumes on the way in which class relations are lived.[3]

The more sociology is presented as a hyper-empiricism, the easier is its integration into Marxism. Alone it would congeal in essentialism and discontinuity. Recovered—as the *moment* of a closely watched empiricism—in the movement of historical totalization, it will find again its profundity and its life. It will be sociology which will maintain the relative irreducibility of social fields, which will bring out—at the heart of the general movement—the resistances, the checks, the ambiguities, the uncertainties. Furthermore, there is no question of adding a method onto Marxism. The very development of the dialectical philosophy must lead it to produce—in a single act—the horizontal synthesis and the totalization in depth. So long as Marxism refuses to do it, others will attempt the coup in its place.

In other words, we reproach contemporary Marxism for throwing over to the side of chance all the concrete determinations of human life and for not preserving

---

[3] This does not mean that the class struggle is less violent. Quite the contrary—it is simply different.

anything of historical totalization except its abstract skeleton of universality. The result is that it has entirely lost the meaning of what it is to be a man; to fill in the gaps, it has only the absurd psychology of Pavlov. Against the idealization of philosophy and the dehumanization of man, we assert that the part of chance can and must be reduced to the minimum. When they tell us: "Napoleon as an individual was only an accident; what was necessary was the military dictatorship as the liquidating regime of the Revolution," we are hardly interested; for we had always known that. What we intend to show is that *this* Napoleon was necessary, that the development of the Revolution forged at once the necessity of the dictatorship and the entire personality of the one who was to administer it, and that the historical process provided *General Bonaparte personally* with preliminary powers and with the occasions which allowed him—and him alone—to hasten this liquidation. In short, we are not dealing with an abstract universal, with a situation so poorly defined that several Bonapartes were *possible*, but with a concrete totalization in which *this* real bourgeoisie, made up of real, living men, was to liquidate *this* Revolution and in which *this* Revolution created its own liquidator in the person of Bonaparte, in himself and for himself—that is, for those bourgeois and in his own eyes. Our intention is not, as is too often claimed, to "give the irrational its due," but, on the contrary, to reduce the part of indetermination and non-knowledge, not to reject Marxism in the name of a third path or of an idealist humanism, but to reconquer man within Marxism.

We have just shown that dialectical materialism is reduced to its own skeleton if it does not integrate into itself certain Western disciplines; but this is only a negative demonstration. Our examples have revealed at the heart of this philosophy a lack of any concrete anthropology. But, without a movement, without a real effort at totalization, the givens of sociology and of psychoanalysis will sleep side by side and will not be integrated into "Knowledge." The default of Marxism has led us to attempt this integration ourselves, with the means at our disposal; that is, by definite operations and according to principles which give to our ideology its unique character, principles which we are now going to set forth.

III · THE PROGRESSIVE-

REGRESSIVE METHOD

I HAVE said that we accept without reservation the thesis set forth by Engels in his letter to Marx: "Men themselves make their history but in a given environment which conditions them." However, this text is not one of the clearest, and it remains open to numerous interpretations. How are we to understand that man makes History if at the same time it is History which makes him? Idealist Marxism seems to have chosen the easiest interpretation: entirely determined by prior circumstances—that is, in the final analysis, by economic conditions—man is a passive product, a sum of conditioned reflexes. Being inserted in the social world amidst other equally conditioned inertias, this inert object, with the nature which it has received, contributes to precipitate or to check the "course of the world." It changes society in the way that a bomb, without ceasing to obey the principle of inertia, can destroy a building. In this case there would be no difference between the human agent and the machine. Marx wrote, in fact: "The invention of a new military weapon, the firearm, of necessity modified the whole inner organization of the army, the relationships inside the cadre on the basis of which individuals form an army and which make of the army an organized whole, and finally, the relations between different armies." In short, the advantage here seems to be on the side of the weapon or the tool; their simple appearance overturns everything.

This conception can be summed up by a statement which appeared in the *Courrier européen* (in Saint Petersburg): "Marx considers social evolution to be a natural process governed by laws which do not depend upon the will, the consciousness, or the intention of men, but which, on the contrary, determine them." Marx quotes this passage in the second preface to *Capital*. Does he really accept it as a fair appraisal of his position? It is difficult to say. He compliments the critic for having excellently described *his* method and points out to him that the real problem concerns *the* dialectical method. But he does not comment on the article in detail, and he concludes by noting that the practical bourgeois *is very clearly conscious* of the contradictions in capitalist society, a remark which seems to be the counterpart of his statement in 1860: "[The workers' movement represents] the conscious participation in the historical process which is overturning society." Now one will observe that the statements in the *Courrier européen* contradict not only the passage quoted earlier from *Herr Vogt* but also the famous third thesis of Feuerbach. "The materialist doctrine according to which men are a product of circumstances and of education . . . does not take into account the fact that circumstances are modified precisely by men and that the educator must be himself educated." Either this is a

mere tautology, and we are simply to understand that
the educator himself is a product of circumstances and
of education—which would render the sentence useless
and absurd; or else it is the decisive affirmation of the
irreducibility of human *praxis*. The educator must be
educated; this means that education must be an enterprise.[1]

If one wants to grant to Marxist thought its full complexity, one would have to say that man in a period of
exploitation is *at once both* the product of his own product and a historical agent who can under no circumstances be taken as a product. This contradiction is not
fixed; it must be grasped in the very movement of *praxis*.
Then it will clarify Engels's statement: men make their
history on the basis of real, prior conditions (among
which we would include acquired characteristics, distortions imposed by the mode of work and of life, alienation, etc.), but it is *the men* who make it and not the
prior conditions. Otherwise men would be merely the
vehicles of inhuman forces which through them would
govern the social world. To be sure, these conditions exist, and it is they, they alone, which can furnish a direction and a material reality to the changes which are
in preparation; but the movement of human *praxis* goes
beyond them while conserving them.

Certainly men do not grasp the real measure of what

[1] Marx has stated this thought specifically: to act upon the educator,
it is necessary to act upon the factors which condition him. Thus the
qualities of external determination and those of that synthetic, progressive unity which is human *praxis* are found inseparably connected
in Marxist thought. Perhaps we should maintain that this wish to
transcend the oppositions of externality and internality, of multiplicity
and unity, of analysis and synthesis, of nature and anti-nature, is
actually the most profound theoretical contribution of Marxism. But
these are suggestions to be developed; the mistake would be to think
that the task is an easy one.

they do—or at least its full import must escape them so
long as the Proletariat, the subject of History, will not in
a single movement realize its unity and become conscious of its historical role. But if History escapes me,
this is not because I do not make it; it is because the
other is making it as well. Engels—who has left us many
hardly compatible statements on this subject—has
shown in *The War of the Peasants,* at any rate, the
meaning which he attached to this contradiction. After
emphasizing the courage and passion of the German
peasants, the justice of their demands, the genius of certain of their leaders (especially Münzer), the intelligence and competence of the revolutionary elite, he
concludes: "In the War of the Peasants, only the princes
had anything to gain; therefore this was its result. They
won not only relatively, since their rivals (the clergy,
the nobility, the city) found themselves weakened, but
also absolutely, since they carried off the best spoils
from the other orders." What was it then which *stole* the
praxis of the rebels? Simply their separation, which had
as its source a definite historical condition—the division
of Germany. The existence of numerous provincial
movements which never succeeded in uniting with one
another, where each one, *other* than the others, acted
differently—this was enough to make each group lose
the real meaning of its enterprise. This does not mean
that the enterprise *as a real action of man upon history*
does not exist, but only that the result achieved, when
it is placed in the totalizing movement, is radically different from the way it appears locally—*even when the
result conforms with the objective proposed.* Finally,
the division of the country caused the war to fail, and
the war resulted only in aggravating and consolidating
this division.

Thus man makes History; this means that he objectifies himself in it and is alienated in it. In this sense History, which is the proper work of *all* activity and of *all* men, appears to men as a foreign force exactly insofar as they do not recognize the meaning of their enterprise (even when locally successful) in the total, objective result. By making a separate peace, the peasants of a certain province won—*so far as they were concerned*. But they weakened their class, and its defeat was to be turned back against them when the landholders, sure of their strength, would deny their pledges. Marxism in the nineteenth century is a gigantic attempt not only to make History but to get a grip on it, practically and theoretically, by uniting the workers' movement and by clarifying the Proletariat's action through an understanding both of the capitalist process and of the workers' objective reality. At the end of this effort, by the unification of the exploited and by the progressive reduction of the number of classes in the struggle, History was finally to have a meaning for man. By becoming conscious of itself, the Proletariat becomes the subject of History; that is, it must recognize itself in History. Even in the everyday struggle the working class must obtain results conforming to the objective aimed at, the consequences of which will at least never be turned back against it.

We are not at this point yet. There is more than one Proletariat, simply because there are national production groups which have developed differently. Not to recognize the solidarity of these Proletariats would be as absurd as to underestimate their *separation*. It is true that the violent divisions and their theoretical consequences (the decay of bourgeois ideology, the temporary arrest of Marxism) force our period to make itself without knowing itself. On the other hand, although we are more than ever subject to these limitations, it is not true that History appears to us as an entirely alien force. Each day with our own hands we make it something other than what we believe we are making it, and History, backfiring, makes us other than we believe ourselves to be or to become. Yet it is less opaque than it was. The Proletariat has discovered and released "its secret"; the capitalist movement is conscious of itself, both as the result of the capitalists' own self-study and through the research carried on by theoreticians in the workers' movement. For each one, the multiplicity of groups, their contradictions and their separations, appear *situated* within more profound unifications. Civil war, colonial war, foreign war, are manifested to all, under cover of the usual mythologies, as different and complementary forms of a single class struggle. It is true that the majority of socialist countries *do not know themselves;* and yet de-Stalinization—as the example of Poland shows—is *also* a progress toward the attainment of awareness. Thus the plurality of *the meanings* of History can be discovered and posited for itself only upon the ground of a future totalization—in terms of the future totalization and in contradiction with it. It is our theoretical and practical duty to bring this totalization closer every day. All is still obscure, and yet everything is in full light. To tackle the theoretical aspect, we have the instruments; we can establish the method. Our historical task, at the heart of this polyvalent world, is to bring closer the moment when History will have *only one meaning*, when it will tend to be dissolved in the concrete men who will make it in common.[2]

[2] It is relatively easy to foresee to what extent every attempt (even that of *a group*) will be posited as a particular determination at the

THE PROJECT

THUS alienation can modify the *results* of an action but not its profound reality. We refuse to confuse the alienated man with a thing or alienation with the physical laws governing external conditions. We affirm the specificity of the human act, which cuts across the social milieu while still holding on to its determinations, and which transforms the world on the basis of given conditions. For us man is characterized above all by his going beyond a situation, and by what he succeeds in making of what he has been made—even if he never recognizes himself in his objectification. This going beyond we find at the very root of the human—in *need*. It is need which, for example, links the scarcity of women in the Marquesas, as a structural fact of the group, and polyandry as a matrimonial institution. For this scarcity is not a simple lack; in its most naked form it expresses a situation in society and contains already an effort to go beyond it. The most rudimentary behavior must be determined both in relation to the real and present factors which condition it and in relation to a certain object, still to come, which it is trying to bring into being.[3] This is what we call *the project*.

heart of the totalizing movement and thereby will achieve results opposed to those which it sought: this will be *a* method, *a* theory, etc. But one can also foresee how its partial aspect will later be broken down by a new generation and how, within the Marxist philosophy, it will be integrated in a wider totality. To this extent even, one may say that the rising generations are more capable of *knowing* (*savoir*)— at least formally—what they are doing than the generations which have preceded us.

[3] Failing to develop by real investigations, Marxism makes use of an arrested dialectic. Indeed, it achieves the totalization of human activities within a homogeneous and infinitely divisible continuum which is nothing other than the "time" of Cartesian rationalism. This temporal

Starting with the project, we define a double simultaneous relationship. In relation to the given, the *praxis* is negativity; but what is always involved is the negation of a negation. In relation to the object aimed at, *praxis* is positivity, but this positivity opens onto the "nonexistent," to what *has not yet* been. A flight and a leap ahead, at once a refusal and a realization, the project retains and unveils the surpassed reality which is refused by the very movement which surpassed it. Thus knowing is a moment of *praxis*, even its most fundamental one; but this knowing does not partake of an absolute Knowledge. Defined by the negation of the refused reality in the name of the reality to be produced, it remains the captive of the action which it clarifies, and disappears along with it. Therefore it is perfectly accurate to say that man is the product of his product. The structures of a society which is created by

environment is not unduly confining when the problem is to examine the process of capitalism, because it is exactly that temporality which capitalist economy produces as the signification of production, of monetary circulation, of the redistribution of property, of credit, of "compound interest." Thus it can be considered a product of the system. But the description of this universal container as a phase of social development is one thing and the dialectical determination of *real* temporality (that is, of the true relation of men to their past and their future) is another. Dialectic as a movement of reality collapses if time is not dialectic; that is, if we refuse to recognize a certain action of the future as such. It would be too long to study here the dialectical temporality of history. For the moment, I have wanted only to indicate the difficulties and to formulate the problem. One must understand that neither men nor their activities are *in time*, but that time, as a concrete quality of history, is made by men on the basis of their original temporalization. Marxism caught a glimpse of true temporality when it criticized and destroyed the bourgeois notion of "progress"—which necessarily implies a homogeneous milieu and coordinates which would allow us to situate the point of departure and the point of arrival. But—without ever having said so—Marxism has renounced these studies and preferred to make use of "progress" again for its own benefit.

human work define for each man an objective situation as a starting point; the truth of a man is the nature of his work, and it is his wages. But this truth defines him just insofar as he constantly goes beyond it in his practical activity. (In a popular democracy this may be, for example, by working a double shift or by becoming an "activist" or by secretly resisting the raising of work quotas. In a capitalist society it may be by joining a union, by voting to go on strike, etc.) Now this surpassing is conceivable only as a relation of the existent to its possibles. Furthermore, to say what man "is" is also to say what he can be—and vice versa. The material conditions of his existence circumscribe the field of his possibilities (his work is too hard, he is too tired to show any interest in union or political activity). Thus the field of possibles is the goal toward which the agent surpasses his objective situation. And this field in turn depends strictly on the social, historical reality. For example, in a society where everything is bought, the possibilities of culture are practically eliminated for the workers if food absorbs 50 per cent or more of their budget. The freedom of the bourgeois, on the contrary, consists in the possibility of his allotting an always increasing part of his income to a great variety of expenditures. Yet the field of possibles, however reduced it may be, always exists, and we must not think of it as a zone of indetermination, but rather as a strongly structured region which depends upon all of History and which includes its own contradictions. It is by transcending the given toward the field of possibles and by realizing one possibility from among all the others that the individual objectifies himself and contributes to making History. The project then takes on a reality which the agent himself may not know, one which, through the conflicts it manifests and engenders, influences the course of events.

Therefore we must conceive of the possibility as doubly determined. On the one side, it is at the very heart of the particular action, the presence of the future as *that which is lacking* and that which, by its very absence, reveals reality. On the other hand, it is the real and permanent future which the collectivity forever maintains and transforms. When common needs bring about the creation of new offices (for example, the multiplication of physicians in a society which is becoming industrialized), these offices, not yet filled—or vacant as the result of retirement or death—constitute for certain people a real, concrete, and *possible* future. These persons *can* go into medicine. This career is not closed to them; at this moment their life lies open before them until death. All things being equal, the professions of army doctor, country doctor, colonial doctor, etc., are characterized by certain advantages and certain obligations which they will quickly know. This future, to be sure, is only partly true; it presupposes a *status quo* and a minimum of order (barring accidents) which is contradicted precisely by the fact that our societies are in constant process of making history. But neither is it false, since it is this—in other words, the interests of the profession, of class, etc., the ever-increasing division of labor, etc.—which first manifests the present contradictions of society. The future is presented, then, as a schematic, always open possibility and as an immediate action on the present.

Conversely, this future defines the individual in his present reality; the conditions which the medical students must fulfill in a bourgeois society *at the same time* reveal the society, the profession, and the social situation of the one who will meet these conditions. If it is still necessary for parents to be well-off, if the practice of giving scholarships is not widespread, then the future doctor appears in his own eyes as a member of the moneyed classes. In turn, he becomes aware of his class by means of the future which it makes possible for him; that is, through his chosen profession. In contrast, for the man who does not meet the required conditions, medicine becomes his *lack*, his *non-humanity* (all the more so as many other careers are "closed" to him at the same time). It is from this point of view, perhaps, that we ought to approach the problem of relative pauperism. Every man is defined negatively by the sum total of possibles which are impossible for him; that is, by a future more or less blocked off. For the underprivileged classes, each cultural, technical, or material enrichment of society represents a diminution, an impoverishment; the future is almost entirely barred. Thus, both positively and negatively, the social possibles are lived as schematic determinations of the individual future. And the most individual possible is only the internalization and enrichment of a social possible.

A member of the ground crew at an air base on the outskirts of London took a plane and, with no experience as a pilot, flew it across the Channel. He is colored; he is prevented from becoming a member of the flying personnal. This prohibition becomes for him a *subjective* impoverishment, but he immediately goes beyond the subjective to the objective. This denied future reflects to him the fate of his "race" and the racism of the English. The *general* revolt on the part of colored men against colonialists is expressed *in him* by his particular refusal of this prohibition. He affirms that a fu-

ture *possible for whites* is *possible for everyone*. This
political position, of which he doubtless has no clear
awareness, he lives as a personal obsession; aviation
becomes *his* possibility as a *clandestine future*. In fact
he chooses a possibility *already recognized* by the colonialists as existing in the colonized (simply because
they cannot rule it out at the start)—the possibility of
rebellion, of risk, of scandal, of repression. This choice
allows us to understand at the same time his individual
project and the present stage of the struggle of the
colonized against the colonialists (the colored have
gone beyond the moment of passive, dignified resistance, but the group of which this man is a part does
not yet have the means of going beyond individual revolt and terrorism). This young rebel is all the more
individual and *unique* in that the struggle in his country demands, for the time being, individual acts. Thus
the unique particularity of this person is the internalization of a double future—that of the whites and that of
his brothers; the contradiction is cloaked and surmounted in a project which launches it toward a brief,
dazzling future, *his* future, shattered immediately by
prison or by accidental death.

What makes American culturism and Kardiner's
theory appear mechanistic and outmoded is the fact
they never conceive of cultural behavior and basic attitudes (or roles, etc.) within the true, living perspective,
which is temporal, but rather conceive of them as past
determinations ruling men in the way that a cause rules
its effects. Everything changes if one considers that
society is presented to each man as *a perspective of the
future* and that this future penetrates to the heart of
each one as a real motivation for his behavior. That the
Marxists allow themselves to be duped by mechanistic

materialism is inexcusable, since they know and approve of large-scale socialist planning. For a man in China the future is more true than the present. So long as one has not studied the structures of the future in a defined society, one necessarily runs the risk of not understanding anything whatsoever about the social.

I cannot describe here the true dialectic of the subjective and the objective. One would have to demonstrate the joint necessity of "the internalization of the external" and "the externalization of the internal." *Praxis*, indeed, is a passage from objective to objective through internalization. The project, as the subjective surpassing of objectivity toward objectivity, and stretched between the objective conditions of the environment and the objective structures of the field of possibles, represents *in itself* the moving unity of subjectivity and objectivity, those cardinal determinants of activity. The subjective appears then as a necessary moment in the objective process. If the material conditions which govern human relations are to become real conditions of *praxis*, they must be lived in the particularity of particular situations. The diminution of buying power would never provoke the workers to make economic demands if they did not feel the diminution in their flesh in the form of a need or of a fear based on bitter experiences. The practice of union action can increase the importance and the efficacy of objective significations among the experienced party militants; the wage scale and the price index can by themselves clarify or motivate their action. But all this objectivity refers ultimately to a lived reality. The worker knows what he has resented and what others will resent. Now, to resent is already to go beyond, to move toward the possibility of an objective transformation. In the *lived experience,* the subjectivity turns back upon itself and wrenches itself from despair by means of *objectification.* Thus the subjective contains within itself the objective, which it denies and which it surpasses toward a new objectivity; and this new objectivity by virtue of *objectification* externalizes the internality of the project as an objectified subjectivity. This means *both* that the lived as such finds its place in the result and that the projected meaning of the action appears in the reality of the world that it may get its truth in the process of totalization.[4]

[4] I add these observations: (1) That this objective truth of the objectified subjective must be considered as the only truth of the subjective. Since the latter exists only in order to be objectified, it is on the basis of the objectification—that is, on the realization—that it must be judged in itself and in the world. An action cannot be judged by the intention behind it. (2) That this truth will allow us to evaluate the *objectified project* in the total picture. An action, such as it appears in the light of contemporary history and of a particular set of circumstances, may be shown to be ill-fated from the start—for the group which supports it (or for some wider formation, a class or a fragment of a class, of which this group forms a part). And at the same time its unique objective characteristic may reveal it to be *an enterprise in good faith.* When one considers an action harmful to the establishing of socialism, it may be so only in relation to this particular aim. To characterize it as harmful can *in no case* prejudice what the action is in itself; that is, considered on another level of objectivity and related to particular circumstances and to the conditioning of the individual environment. People often set up a dangerous distinction: an act may be objectively *blameworthy* (by the Party, by the Cominform, etc.) while remaining *subjectively acceptable.* A person could be subjectively of good will, objectively a traitor. This distinction testifies to an advanced disintegration in Stalinist thought; that is, in voluntaristic idealism. It is easy to see that it goes back to that "petit bourgeois" distinction between the good intentions with which "hell is paved," etc., and their real consequences. In fact, the general import of the action considered and its individual signification are equally *objective* characteristics (since they are interpreted within an objectivity), and they both engage subjectivity (since they are its objectification) whether within the total movement which discovers it as it is *from the point of view of the totalization* or within a particular synthesis. Furthermore, an act has many other levels of truth, and these levels do not represent a dull hierarchy, but a complex movement of

Only the project, as a mediation between two moments of objectivity, can account for history; that is, for human *creativity*. It is necessary to choose. In effect: either we reduce everything to identity (which amounts to substituting a mechanistic materialism for dialectical materialism)—or we make of dialectic a celestial law which imposes itself on the Universe, a metaphysical force which by itself engenders the historical process (and this is to fall back into Hegelian idealism)—or we restore to the individual man his power to go beyond his situation by means of work and action. This solution alone enables us to base the movement of totalization *upon the real*. We must look for dialectic in the relation of men with nature, with "the starting conditions," and in the relation of men with one another. There is where

---

contradictions which are posited and surpassed; for example, the totalization which appraises the act in its relation to historical *praxis* and to the conjuncture of circumstances is itself denounced as an abstract, incomplete totalization (a *practical* totalization) insofar as it has not turned back to the action to reintegrate it *also* as a uniquely individual attempt. The condemnation of the insurgents at Kronstadt was perhaps inevitable; it was perhaps the judgment of history on this tragic attempt. But at the same time this practical judgment (the only real one) will remain that of an enslaved history so long as it does not include the free interpretation of the revolt in terms of the insurgents themselves and of the contradictions of the moment. This free interpretation, someone may say, is in no way *practical* since the insurgents, as well as their judges, are dead. But that is not true. The historian, by consenting to study facts at all levels of reality, liberates future history. This liberation can come about, as a visible and efficacious action, only within the compass of the general movement of democratization; but conversely it cannot fail to accelerate this movement. (3) In the world of alienation, the historical agent never entirely recognizes himself in his act. This does not mean that historians should not recognize him in it precisely *as* an alienated man. However this may be, alienation is at the base and at the summit; and the agent never undertakes anything which is not the negation of alienation and which does not fall back into an alienated world. But the alienation of the objectified result is not the same as the alienation at the point of departure. It is the passage from the one to the other which defines the person.

it gets its start, *resulting* from the confrontation of projects. The characteristics of the human project alone enable us to understand that this result is a new reality provided with its own signification instead of remaining simply a statistical mean.[5] It is impossible to develop these considerations here. They will be the subject of Part Two of *Critique of Dialectical Reason*. I limit myself here to three observations which will at least permit us to consider this presentation a brief formulation of the problems of existentialism.

· 1 ·

THE GIVEN, which we surpass at every instant by the simple fact of living it, is not restricted to the material conditions of our existence; we must include in it, as I have said, our own childhood. What was once both a vague comprehension of our class, of our social conditioning by way of the family group, and a blind going beyond, an awkward effort to wrench ourselves away from all this, at last ends up inscribed in us in the form

[5] On exactly this point Engels's thought seems to have wavered. We know the unfortunate use which he sometimes makes of this idea of a *mean*. His evident purpose is to remove from dialectic its a priori character as an unconditioned force. But then dialectic promptly disappears. It is impossible to conceive of the appearance of systematic processes such as capitalism or colonialism if we consider the resultants of antagonistic forces to be means. We must understand that individuals do not collide like molecules, but that, upon the basis of given conditions and divergent and opposed interests, each one understands and surpasses the project of the other. It is by these surpassings and surpassings of surpassings that a social object may be constituted which, taken as a whole, is a reality *provided with meaning and something* in which nobody can completely recognize himself; in short, *a human work without an author. Means,* as Engels and statisticians conceive of them, suppress the author, but by the same stroke they suppress the work and its "humanity." We shall have the opportunity to develop this idea in Part Two of the *Critique.*

of *character*. At this level are found the learned gestures (bourgeois gestures, socialist gestures) and the contradictory roles which compose us and which tear us apart (e.g., for Flaubert, the role of dreamy, pious child, and that of future surgeon, the son of an atheistic surgeon). At this level also are the traces left by our first revolts, our desperate attempts to go beyond a stifling reality, and the resulting deviations and distortions. To surpass all that is also to preserve it. We shall think *with* these original deviations, we shall act *with* these gestures which we have learned and which we want to reject. By projecting ourselves toward our possible so as to escape the contradictions of our existence, we unveil them, and they are revealed in our very action although this action is richer than they are and gives us access to a social world in which new contradictions will involve us in new conduct. Thus we can say both that we constantly surpass our class and that our class reality is made manifest by means of this very surpassing. The realization of the possible necessarily results in the production of an object or an event in the social world; this realization is then our *objectification,* and the original contradictions which are reflected there testify to our *alienation*.

By now one can understand that capitalism is expressed through the mouth of the bourgeois but that the bourgeois does not thereby stop speaking of anything else. In fact, he speaks of all sorts of things; he speaks of his tastes in food, his artistic preferences, his hates and his loves, all of which as such are irreducible to the economic process and are developed in accordance with their own contradictions. But the universal, abstract signification of these particular propositions is indeed capital and nothing else. It is true that this industrialist on vacation throws himself frantically into hunting, into underwater fishing, *in order to forget* his professional and economic activities; it is true also that this passionate waiting for fish or for game has in his case a meaning which only psychoanalysis can let us know. But the fact still remains that the material conditions of the act constitute it objectively as "expressing capital" and that, in addition, this act itself by its economic repercussions is integrated in the capitalist process. Thus it makes history statistically at the level of relations of production because it contributes to maintaining the existing social structures. But these consequences must not deter us from taking the act at various more and more concrete levels and examining the consequences which it can have at these levels. From this point of view, every act, every word, has a hierarchized multiplicity of significations. In this pyramid the lower and more general signification serves as a supporting framework for the higher and more concrete signification; but although the latter can never get outside the framework, it is impossible to deduce the concrete from the general or to dissolve the concrete in the general. For example, the practice of economic Malthusianism on the part of the French employer involves in certain circles of our bourgeoisie a marked tendency toward avarice. But if one tried to see in the avarice of a particular group or person only the simple result of economic Malthusianism, one would fail to discover the concrete reality. For avarice stems from the earliest years of childhood when the child scarcely knows what money is. It is therefore *also* a defiant way of living his own body and his own situation in the world; and it is a relation to death. The correct procedure is to study these concrete characteristics *against the background* of the economic movement but without misunderstanding their specific nature.[6] It is only in this way that we shall be able to direct ourselves toward the *totalization*.

This does not mean that the material condition (here French economic Malthusianism, the type of investments which it determines, the tightening of credit, etc.) is insufficiently "determining" as related to the attitude considered. Or, if you prefer, there is no need to add to it any other *factor*, provided that one studies on all levels the reciprocal action of the facts which the material condition engenders by way of the human project. Malthusianism can be lived by the son of a "small businessman"—that archaic category which our

[6] In *L'Esprit*, in an issue devoted to medicine, Jean Marcenac criticizes certain journalists for giving in to their "personalist" tendencies and dwelling at length on the relation between doctor and patient. He adds that the reality is "more humbly" and more simply economic. ("Lettres françaises," March 7, 1957.) Here is an excellent example of the prejudices which sterilize Marxist intellectuals in the French Communist Party. That the practice of medicine in France is conditioned by the capitalist structure of our society and by the historical circumstances which have brought us to Malthusianism, nobody will deny. It is evident too that the relative scarcity of doctors is the result of our system of government and that it affects in turn the doctor's relation with his patients. And we will admit that in the majority of cases the sick man is only a *patient* and that there is competition among the physicians who may take care of him, and that this economic relation, based on "relations of production," enters in to change the nature of the direct relation and even in a certain way to reify it. What then? In a great number of cases, these factors condition, transform, and change the nature of the human relation. They disguise it, but they cannot remove from it its original quality. Within the limits which I have just described and under the influence of the factors already set forth, the fact remains that we are not dealing with a wholesale dealer in his relations with a retail merchant, nor with a private soldier in his relations with a superior officer, but with a man who, inside our political system, is defined by the *material* enterprise of healing. This enterprise has a double aspect: There is no doubt—to use Marx's terms—that it is the sick man who creates the doctor. And in one respect, the illness is social, not only because it is often occupational, nor because it expresses by itself a certain level of life, but also because society—for a given state of medical techniques—

Malthusians still hold on to for support—in the poverty
and insecurity of his family and as the perpetual necessity of calculating, of economizing, penny by penny.
Although very often the father is merely his own em-
ployee, the child may discover in him an attachment to
property which becomes the more violent as the property is the more threatened. Under certain circumstances, the child may experience the struggle against
death as another aspect of this rage to possess. But this
immediate relation to death, which the father flees in
the owning of property, comes precisely from the owned
property itself inasmuch as it is lived as the internalization of the radical external. The specific characteristics

---

decides its sick and its dead. But in another respect, it is a certain
manifestation—a particularly urgent one—of the material life, of
needs, and of death. It therefore confers on the doctor whom it produces a specific and particularly profound connection with other men
who are themselves in a well-defined situation (they suffer, they are
in danger, they have need of help). This social and material relation is
affirmed in practice as a bond even more intimate than the sexual act;
but this intimacy is realized only by activities and precise, original
techniques engaging both persons. That it is radically different according to circumstances (in socialized medicine or where medical
service is paid for by the patient) does not in any way alter the fact
that in both cases we find a real, specific, *human relation* and—even
in capitalist countries, at least in a great number of cases—a person-
to-person relation, conditioned by the medical techniques and surpassing them toward its own end. Doctor and patient form a couple
united by a common enterprise. The one must heal and care for; the
other must be taken care of, be healed. This cannot be done without
mutual confidence.

Marx refused to dissolve this reciprocity in the economic. To state
its limits and its conditions, to demonstrate its possible reification, to
observe that manual workers create the conditions of material existence
for intellectual workers (and consequently of the doctor)—does this
change the practical necessity of studying *today* and *in the bourgeois
democracies* the problems of this indissoluble couple, of this complex,
human, real, and totalizing relation? What contemporary Marxists
have forgotten is that man, alienated, mystified, reified, etc., still remains a man. When Marx speaks of reification, he does not mean to
show that we are transformed into things but that we are men condemned to live humanly the condition of material things.

of the thing possessed, felt as the separation of men and the solitude of the property owner facing his own death, condition his will to tighten the bonds of possession; that is, to find his survival in the very object which announces to him his disappearance. The child may discover, surpass, and conserve, in a single movement, the anxiety of the owner on the brink of ruin and of the man, a prey to death. Between them, the child will realize a new mediation which may be precisely avarice. These different moments in the life of the father or of the family group have as their common source relations of production apprehended through the movement of the French economy. But they are lived in different ways because the same person (and with still greater reason, the group) is situated at different levels in relation to that unique but complex source (employer, producer—he often works himself—consumer, etc.). In the child these moments come into contact, modify one another within the unity of a single project, and thereby constitute a new reality.

There are a few further points which we ought to note. In the first place, we must remember that we live our childhood as our *future*. Our childhood determines gestures and roles in the perspective of what is to come. This is not a matter of the mechanical reappearance of montages. Since the gestures and roles are inseparable from the project which transforms them, they are relations independent of the terms which they unite and which we must find at every moment of the human enterprise. Surpassed and maintained, they constitute what I shall call the internal coloration of the project; in saying this I distinguish them as much from motivations as from specifications. The motivation of the enterprise is one with the enterprise itself; the specification

and the project are one and the same reality. Finally
the project never has any *content*, since its objectives
are at once united with it and yet transcendent. But its
coloration—i.e., subjectively, its taste; objectively, its
style—is nothing but the surpassing of our original
deviations. This surpassing is not an instantaneous
movement, it is a long work; each moment of this work
is at once the surpassing and, to the extent that it is
posited for itself, the pure and simple subsistence of
these deviations at a given level of integration. For this
reason a life develops in spirals; it passes again and
again by the same points but at different levels of integration and complexity.

As a child, Flaubert feels that he is deprived of pa-
ternal affection because of his older brother. Achille resembles the father Flaubert; in order to please his
father, Gustave would have to imitate Achille; in sulky
resentment the child refuses to do so. When he enters
college, Gustave finds the situation unchanged. Nine
years earlier, Achille, a brilliant student, has already
won all the first places and earned the approval of the
chief physician. If his younger brother hopes to win
the esteem of his father, he must get the same grades
for the same assignments as his older brother. He refuses without even formulating his refusal. This means
that an unrecognized resistance hampers him in his
work. He will be an *average* student, which, in the
Flaubert household, is a disgrace. This second situation
is nothing other than the first one further restricted by
the new factor, which is the college. Gustave's contacts
with his fellow students are not *dominant* conditions;
the family problem is so serious for him that he is not
concerned about other relations. If he is humiliated by
the success of certain of his fellow students, it is *solely*

because their honors confirm the superiority of Achille (who took the prize for excellence in every class). The third moment comes when Flaubert consents to study law; in order to be sure of being *different* from Achille, he decides to be inferior to him. He will hate his future career as the proof of this inferiority; he will launch into an idealist overcompensation and finally, faced with becoming an attorney, he will get himself out of it by attacks of "hysteria." This third moment is an enrichment and a further restriction of the initial conditions. Each phase, isolated, seems to be a repetition; the movement proceeding from childhood to nervous breakdowns is, on the contrary, a perpetual surpassing of these givens. The end product is Gustave Flaubert's commitment to literature.[7]

But *at the same time* that these givens are a past-surpassed, they appear in every operation as a past-surpassing—that is, as a future. *Our roles are always future.* They appear to each one as tasks to be performed, ambushes to be avoided, powers to be exercised, etc. It may be that "paternity" is a role—as certain American sociologists claim. It may be also that a particular young married man hopes to become a father in order to be identified with or to substitute himself for his own father, or, on the other hand, to free himself of his father by assuming his father's "attitude." In any case, this past relation with his parents (or at least a relation which has been lived profoundly in the past) manifests itself to him only as the line of flight in a new enterprise. Paternity opens to him a life until his death. If it is a role, it is a role which one in-

[7] One will guess immediately that Flaubert's real problems were more complex than this. I have "schematized" outrageously, my intention being only to demonstrate the permanence underlying the continuous alteration.

vents, which one does not cease to learn again under circumstances always new, and which one hardly knows until the moment of death. Complexes, the style of life, and the revelation of the past-surpassing as a future to be created are one and the same reality. It is the project as an *oriented life,* as man's affirmation through action. And at the same time it is that mist of irrationality which cannot be located, which is reflected from the future in our childhood memories and from our childhood in our rational choices as mature men.[8]

The second observation which we should make refers to the totalization as a movement of History and as a theoretical and practical attempt to "situate" an event, a group, or a man. I have remarked earlier that a single act can be evaluated at more and more complex levels and that consequently it is expressed by a series of very diverse significations. One should not conclude, as certain philosophers do, that these significations remain independent, separated, so to speak, by impassable distances. Of course, the Marxist is not generally guilty of this fault. He shows how the significations of superstructures are produced in terms of substructures. He may go further and show—along with their autonomy —the symbolic function of certain practices or certain superstructural beliefs. But this cannot suffice for the *totalization,* as a dialectical process of revelation. The superimposed significations are isolated and enumerated by analysis. The movement which has joined them together *in life* is, on the contrary, synthetic. The conditioning remains the same; therefore neither the importance of the factors nor their order is changed. But we will lose sight of human reality if we do not consider the significations as synthetic, multidimensional, indis-

[8] Irrationality *for us,* of course, not *in itself.*

soluble objects, which hold individual places in a space-time with multiple dimensions. The mistake here is to reduce the lived signification to the simple linear statement which language gives it.

We have seen that the individual revolt of the "airplane thief" is a particularization of the collective revolt of the colonized; at the same time it is in addition, by its very incarnation, an emancipating act. We must understand that this complex relation between the collective revolt and the individual obsession can neither be reduced to a metaphorical bond nor dissolved in generality. The concrete presence of the object of the obsession (the *airplane*), the practical concerns (how to get into it; when; etc.) are irreducibles. This man did not want to make a political demonstration; he was concerned with his individual destiny. But we know also that what he *was doing* (the collective demand, the emancipating scandal) had to be implicitly contained by what he *believed himself to be doing* (what, moreover, he *was doing*, too, for he stole the plane, he piloted it, and he was killed in France). It is impossible, then, to separate these two significations or to reduce one to the other; they are two inseparable faces of a single object. And here is a third: the relation to death; that is, the refusal and assumption, both together, of a forbidden future. This death expresses at the same time the impossible revolt of his people, hence his *actual* relation with the colonizers, the radical totality of his hate and refusal, and finally the inward project of this man—his choice of a brief, dazzling freedom, of a freedom to die. These various aspects of the relation to death are in turn united and are irreducible to one another. They bestow new dimensions on the act. At the same time they reflect the relation to the colonizers and the obsessional relation to the object—that is, the dimensions earlier unveiled—and they are reflected in these dimensions; these determinations contain and collect together within themselves the revolt by death and the freedom to die.[9] Naturally we are lacking certain other information; we do not know just what childhood, what experience, what material conditions, characterize the man and color the project. There is no doubt, however, that each one of these determinations would add its own richness, would contain the others within itself. (Whatever the childhood may have been, was it not the apprenticeship for this desperate condition, for this future without a future, etc.? The line from death to childhood is so narrow, so rapid in all of us, that we too may ask ourselves whether there has not been since our first years a project of bearing-witness-to-die, etc.) By a particular illumination, each of these determinations would demonstrate to us its own existence in the other significations, as a collapsed presence, as the irrational bond between certain signs, etc. And do we not believe that the very materiality of life is there too as a fundamental condition and as an objective signification of all these significations? The novelist will show us first one, then the other of these dimensions as thoughts alternating in the "mind" of his hero. But the novelist will be lying. It is not thoughts which are involved (at least not necessarily), and all are given together, not one at a time. The man is locked up *inside;* he does not cease to be bound by *all* these walls which enclose him or to *know* that he is immured. All of these walls make *a single prison,* and this prison is *a single life, a single act.*

[9] Let no one speak here of *symbolization.* That is quite another thing: his stealing the plane *is* death; his thinking of death *is* for him *this* plane.

Each signification is transformed, continues to be transformed, and its transformation has repercussions on all the others. What the totalization must discover therefore is the multidimensional *unity* of the act.

Our ancient habits of thought risk oversimplifying this unity, a condition of both reciprocal interpenetration and the relative autonomy of significations. The present form of language is hardly fit to restore it. Yet it is with these poor means and these bad habits that we must try to render the complex, polyvalent unity of these facets, as the dialectical law of their correspondences (that is, of the connections of each one with each other and of each one with all). The dialectical knowing of man, according to Hegel and Marx, demands a new rationality. Because nobody has been willing to establish this rationality within experience, I state as a fact—absolutely no one, either in the East or in the West, writes or speaks a sentence or a word about us and our contemporaries that is not a gross error.[1]

· 2 ·

THE project must of necessity cut across the field of instrumental possibilities.[2] The particular quality of the

[1] Come now, someone will object, hasn't anyone ever said anything true? Quite the contrary. So long as thought watches over its own movement, all is truth or a moment of truth. Even mistakes contain some real knowing. Condillac's philosophy in his century, in the current which carried the bourgeoisie toward revolution and liberalism, was much more true—as a real factor in historical evolution—than Jaspers's philosophy is today. The false is death. Our present ideas are false because they have died before us. There are some which reek of carrion and others which are very clean little skeletons; it amounts to the same thing.

[2] Actually the "social fields" are numerous and vary with the society considered. It is not my purpose to furnish a nomenclature for them. I am choosing one of them in order to demonstrate the process of surpassing in particular instances.

instruments transforms it more or less profoundly; they condition the objectification. Now the instrument itself, whatever it may be, is the product of a certain development of techniques and, in the final analysis, of the productive forces. Since our theme is philosophical, I shall take my examples from the cultural sphere. It must be understood that whatever an ideological project may be in appearance, its ultimate goal is to change the basic situation by becoming aware of its contradictions. Sprung from a particular conflict which expresses the universality of class and condition, it aims at surpassing it in order to reveal it, to reveal it in order to make it manifest to all, to manifest it in order to resolve it. But between the simple revelation and the public manifestation, there is interposed a field restricted and defined by cultural instruments and by language. The development of productive forces conditions scientific knowledge, which in turn conditions it. The relations of production, through this knowledge, outline the lineaments of a philosophy; the concrete and lived history gives birth to particular systems of ideas which, within the framework of this philosophy, express the real and practical attitudes of defined social groups.[3] These words are charged with new significa-

[3] Desanti demonstrates well how the mathematical rationalism of the eighteenth century, sustained by mercantile capitalism and the development of credit, leads to conceiving of space and time as homogeneous, infinite milieux. Consequently, God, who was immediately present to the medieval world, falls outside of the world, becomes the hidden God. In another Marxist work Goldmann shows how Jansenism, which at its heart is a theory of the absence of God and the tragedy of life, reflects the contradictory passion which overthrows the *noblesse de robe*, supplanted in the King's favor by a new bourgeoisie and unable either to accept its fall from grace or to revolt against the monarch from whom it derived its sustenance. These two interpretations—which make one think of Hegel's "panlogicism" and "pantragicism"—are complementary. Desanti points to the cultural

tions; their universal meaning is narrowed and deep-
ened. The word "Nature" in the eighteenth century
creates an immediate complicity among those who question it. We are not speaking here of a strict signification,
and they never left off discussing the Idea of Nature
at the time of Diderot. But this philosophical motif, this
theme, was understood by everyone. Thus the general
categories of the culture, the particular systems, and
the language which expresses them are already the objectification of a class, the reflection of conflicts, latent
or declared, and the particular manifestation of alienation. The world is outside; language and culture are
not inside the individual like stamps registered by his
nervous system. It is the individual who is inside culture
and inside language; that is, inside a special section of
the field of instruments. In order to *manifest* what he
uncovers, he therefore has at his disposal elements both
too rich and too few. Too few: words, types of reason-
ing, methods, exist only in limited quantity; among
them there are empty spaces, lacunae, and his growing
thought cannot find its appropriate expression. Too
rich: each vocable brings along with it the profound
signification which the whole epoch has given to it.
As soon as the ideologist speaks, he says more and
something different from what he wants to say; the
period steals his thought from him. He constantly veers
about, and the idea finally expressed is a profound
deviation; he is caught in the mystification of words.

The Marquis de Sade, as Simone de Beauvoir has
shown, lived the decline of a feudal system, all of whose
privileges were being challenged, one by one. His

---

field; Goldmann points to the determination of one part of this field by
a human passion experienced concretely by a particular group upon
the occasion of its historic fall.

famous "sadism" is a blind attempt to reaffirm in violence his rights as a warrior, founding them on the subjective *quality* of his person. Now this attempt is already permeated with bourgeois subjectivism; objective titles of nobility are replaced by an untrammeled superiority on the part of the Ego. From the beginning his impulse toward violence is deviated. But when he wants to go further, he finds himself face to face with the essential Idea: the Idea of Nature. He wants to show that the law of Nature is the law of the strongest, that massacres and tortures only reproduce natural destructions, etc.[4] But the Idea contains one meaning which throws him off: in the eyes of everyone living in 1789, aristocrat or bourgeois, Nature is good. Suddenly the whole system is going to move off course; since murder and torture can only imitate Nature, this is because the most heinous crimes are good and the finest virtues wicked. At exactly this point, our aristocrat is won over by revolutionary ideas; he experiences the contradiction of all the nobles who had been preparing since 1787 what is called today "the aristocratic revolution." He is at once both victim (he suffered from the *lettres de cachet* and spent years in the Bastille) and privileged. This contradiction, which leads others to the guillotine or to forced emigration, he carries over into revolutionary ideology. He demands freedom (which for him would be freedom to kill) and communication among men (when he seeks to manifest to others his own narrow and profound experience of non-communication). His contradictions, his ancient privileges, and his fall condemn him indeed to solitude. He will see his experience of what Stirner will later call the Unique, stolen and

---

[4] This is already a concession; instead of making Nature his base of operations, an aristocrat sure of his rights would have spoken of Blood.

deviated by the *Universal,* by *rationality,* by *equality,* the concept-tools of his period; it is through these that he will try painfully to think himself. The result of all this is that aberrant ideology: the only relation of person to person is that which binds the torturer and his victim; *at the same time* this conception is the search for communication through the conflicts and the deviated affirmation of absolute non-communication. It is in these terms that he erects a monstrous work which it would be wrong to classify too quickly as one of the last vestiges of aristocratic thought, but which appears rather as the claim of the solitary man, grasped opportunely and transformed by the universalist ideology of the revolutionaries.

This example shows how wrong contemporary Marxism is in neglecting the particular content of a cultural system and reducing it immediately to the universality of a class ideology. A system is an alienated man who wants to go beyond his alienation and who gets entangled in alienated words; it is an achievement of awareness which finds itself deviated by its own instruments and which the culture transforms into a particular *Weltanschauung.* It is at the same time a struggle of thought against its social instruments, an effort to direct them, to empty them of their superfluity, to compel them to express only the thought itself. The consequence of these contradictions is the fact that an ideological system is an irreducible; since the instruments, whatever they are, alienate the one who employs them and modify the meaning of his action, the idea must be considered to be both the objectification of the concrete man and his alienation. The idea is the man himself externalizing himself in the materiality of language. It is important therefore to study it in all its developments, to discover its *subjective* signification (that is, for the one who expresses it) and its intentionality in order to understand its deviations and to pass at last to its objective realization. Thus we will verify the fact that history is "tricky," as Lenin said, and that we underestimate its tricks. We will discover that the majority of the works of the mind are complex objects, difficult to classify, that one can rarely "situate" them in relation to a single class ideology, but rather that they reproduce in their profound structure the contradictions and struggles of contemporary ideologies. We will realize that we must not see in a bourgeois system today the simple negation of revolutionary materialism; on the contrary, we must show how the system responds to the attraction of this philosophy, how the philosophy is included in it, how the attractions and repulsions, influences, gentle forces of insinuation or violent conflicts pursue one another inside each idea, how the idealism of a Western thinker is defined by an arrest of thought, by a refusal to develop certain themes already present —in short, by a sort of incompleteness rather than as a "carnival of subjectivity." Sade's thought is *neither* that of an aristocrat *nor* that of a bourgeois; it is the lived hope of a noble, outlawed by his class, who has found no means of expressing himself except through the dominant concepts of the rising class, and who made use of these concepts by perverting them and by distorting himself through them. In particular, revolutionary universalism, which marks the attempt of the bourgeoisie to manifest itself as the universal class, is completely falsified by Sade to the point of its becoming in him a source of grim humor. It is in this way that this thought, at the very heart of madness, still retains a lively power of debate. By the very use which it makes of them, it contributes to overthrowing the bourgeois ideas of analytical reason, natural goodness, progress, equality, universal harmony. Sade's pessimism joins that of the manual laborer, to whom the bourgeois revolution gave nothing, and who perceived at about 1794 that he was excluded from that "universal" class. It is removed from revolutionary optimism on both sides at once.

Culture is only one example. The ambiguity of political and social action results most often from profound contradictions between the needs, the motives of the act, the immediate project and, on the other side, the collective apparatus of the social field—that is, the instruments of *praxis*. Marx, who spent a long time studying the French Revolution, derived from his study a theoretical principle which we accept: at a certain stage in their development, the productive forces come into conflict with the relations of production, and the period which begins then is revolutionary. There is no doubt, in fact, that commerce and industry were stifled in 1789 by the regulations and particularisms which characterized feudal ownership. Thus we find here the explanation of a certain class conflict, that between the bourgeoisie and the nobility; thus the general structures and the fundamental movement of the French Revolution are determined. But we must observe that the bourgeois class—although industrialization was just beginning—had a clear awareness of its needs and its powers; it was *adult*, it had at its disposal all the technicians, all the techniques, all the tools.

Things are totally different when we want to study a particular moment in that history. For example, the action of the *sans-culottes* against the Commune of Paris and the Convention. The starting point is simple: the people suffered terribly from lack of food; there was *famine and they wanted to eat*. There is the need, there is the motive; and here is the basic project—still general and vague, but immediate—to act upon the authorities so as to obtain a rapid improvement in the situation. This basic situation is revolutionary *on condition that* instruments for action are found and that a policy is defined by the use which will be made of the instruments. Now the group of *sans-culottes* is composed of heterogeneous elements; it joins together petit bourgeois, craftsmen, workers, the majority of whom possess their own tools. This semi-proletarian segment of the Third Estate (one of our historians, Georges Lefebvre, has called it a "Popular Front") remains attached to the system of private property. It would hope to make of the latter a sort of social duty. Hence it intends to limit a commercial freedom that tends to encourage monopolies. Now this ethical conception of bourgeois property does not proceed unequivocally; later it will be one of the favorite mystifications of the imperialistic bourgeoisie. But in 1793 it appears primarily as the residue of a certain feudal, paternalistic concept, which had its birth under the *Ancien Régime*. The relations of production under feudalism found their symbol in the legal thesis of absolute monarchy: the king eminently possesses the land and His Property is identified with the Property of his people; those subjects who are land-holders receive from his bounty the constantly renewed guaranty of their property. In the name of this ambiguous idea, which they remember without recognizing its outmoded character, the *sans-culottes* demand taxation. Now taxation is at the same time a recollection and an anticipation. It is an anticipation; for those groups who are most fully aware demand of the revo-

lutionary government that it sacrifice everything to the
building up and defense of a democratic republic. War
leads necessarily to *economic planning*—that, in one
sense, is what they want to say. But this new demand
is expressed by means of an ancient signification which
twists its direction toward a practice of the hated
monarchy: taxation, price ceilings, control of markets,
public granaries—such were the methods constantly
employed in the eighteenth century to combat famine.
In the program proposed by the people, the Montagnards as well as the Girondists recognize with horror
the authoritarian customs of the regime which they had
just demolished. It is a step backward. Their economists
are unanimous in declaring that only complete freedom
to produce and to trade can bring back abundance.
It has been claimed that the representatives of the bourgeoisie were defending special interests; that is certain,
but it is not the essential. Freedom found its most per-
sistent defenders among the Girondists, who are said
to have represented primarily shipowners, bankers,
international trade. The interests of these upper bourgeois could not be affected by the taxation of grain.
It is claimed, and rightly, that the Montagnards, who
let their hand be forced, were particularly supported
by the purchasers of national properties, who were in
danger of having their profit limited by taxes. Roland,
the sworn enemy of economic planning, held no property. In fact, these members of the Convention, for the
most part poor—intellectuals, lawyers, petty officials—
had an ideological and practical passion for economic
freedom. In it the general interest of the bourgeois class
was objectified; they wished to construct the future
even more than they wanted to manage the present.
In their eyes, free production, free circulation, free com-

petition, were the three indissoluble conditions of progress. Yes, passionately *progressive,* they wanted to advance history, and they advanced it, in fact, by reducing property ownership to the direct relation of the
possessor with the thing possessed.

In these terms everything becomes complex and difficult. How are we to evaluate the meaning of the conflict
objectively? Are these bourgeois moving in the direction
of History when they oppose even the most moderate
economic control? Was an authoritarian war economy
premature? Would it have encountered insurmountable
resistance? [5] Would it have been necessary for capitalism to develop its internal contradictions in order for
certain bourgeois to adopt certain forms of a planned
economy? And the *sans-culottes?* They exercise their
fundamental right in demanding the satisfaction of
their needs. But isn't the method which they propose
going to take them backward? Are they, as some Marxists have dared to say, the rear guard of the Revolution?
It is true that the demand for price ceilings, through
the memories which it awakened, revived the past in the
minds of some of the starving. Forgetting the famines of
the eighties, they cried out: "At the time of the kings,
we had bread." Of course, others took the regulations in
quite a different sense, anticipating through them a
socialism. But this socialism was only a mirage, since
there was no means of realizing it. Furthermore, it was
vague. Baboeuf, said Marx, came too late. Too late and
too soon. On the one side, was it not the people themselves, the people of the *sans-culottes,* who *made* the
Revolution? Wasn't *Thermidor* rendered possible by the
growing dissension between the *sans-culottes* and the

[5] Someone will say that it did encounter *some.* But this is not so
clear; the fact is that it was never really applied.

controlling faction of the members of the Convention? And Robespierre's dream of a nation with neither rich nor poor, where everybody was a property owner— was not that too going against the current? To give first place to the necessities of the struggle against the reaction within, against the armies of the hostile Powers, to realize the bourgeois Revolution fully and to defend it—such was, to be sure, the task, the only task, of the National Convention. But since this Revolution was made *by the people*, was it not necessary to integrate in it the popular demands? At the beginning the famine helped: "If bread had been cheap," writes Georges Lefebvre, "the brutal intervention of the people, which was indispensable for assuring the fall of the *Ancien Régime*, would perhaps not have taken place, and the bourgeoisie would not have triumphed so easily." But starting with the moment when the bourgeoisie overthrew Louis XVI, from the moment when its representatives assumed plenary responsibilities in its name, it was necessary for the popular force to intervene in support of government and institutions, no longer to overthrow them. And how could this aim be accomplished without giving satisfaction to the people?

Thus the situation, the survival of ancient significations, the embryonic development of industry and of the Proletariat, an abstract ideology of universality— all contributed to deviate both the bourgeois action and the popular action. It is true that the people *supported* the Revolution and true, too, that their distress had counter-revolutionary tendencies. It is true that their *political* hatred of the vanished regime varied according to circumstances, tending either to disguise the people's social demands or to give way before them. It is true that no genuine synthesis of the political and the social could be attempted, since the Revolution was in fact paving the way for the advent of bourgeois exploitation. It is true that the bourgeoisie, bent on conquering, was truly the revolutionary avant-garde; but it is true also that it was resolved at the same time to *finish* the Revolution. It is true that by effecting a veritable social upheaval under the pressure of the Radicals, the bourgeoisie would have generalized the civil war and handed the country over to foreigners. But it is true, too, that by discouraging the revolutionary ardor of the people, it was preparing for defeat and the return of the Bourbons at some date sooner or later.

And then it gave in; it voted for the price ceiling. The Montagnards considered this vote a compromise and publicly apologized for it. "We are in a besieged fortress!" This is the first time, to my knowledge, that the myth of the besieged fortress was charged with justifying a revolutionary government's compromise with its principles under pressure of necessity. But the economic regulations seem not to have given the results which were counted on; at bottom, the situation did not change. When the *sans-culottes* return to the Convention on September 5, 1793, they are still hungry, but this time again they lack the requisite instruments. They *are unable* to think that the rise in the price of commodities has general causes due to the system of assignats; that is, to the bourgeois refusal to finance the war by taxes. They still imagine that their misery is brought about by counter-revolutionaries. The petit bourgeois members of the Convention, for their part, cannot incriminate the system without condemning economic liberalism; they too are reduced to invoking enemies. Hence that strange day of dupery when Billaud-Varenne and Robespierre, taking advantage of the fact that the popular delegation demanded the punishment of those responsible, are going to make use of the obscure anger of the people, whose real motives are economic, to support the enforcement of a *political* terror. The people will see heads fall; but it will remain without bread. The controlling bourgeoisie, because it is neither willing nor able to change the system, is going to be decimated itself until *Thermidor*, reaction, and Bonaparte.

We see that it is a struggle in the dark. In each of these groups, the original movement is deviated by the necessities of expression and action, by the objective limitation of the field of instruments (theoretical and practical), by the survival of outdated significations and the ambiguity of new significations (very often, moreover, the second are expressed through the first). Starting here, a task is imposed upon us. This is to recognize the irreducible originality of the social-political groups thus formed and to define them in their very complexity, in terms of their incomplete development and their deviated objectification. We must avoid idealist significations; we will refuse altogether to assimilate the *sans-culottes* to a true Proletariat and to deny the existence of an embryonic Proletariat. We will refuse, save in cases where actual experience imposes it on us, to regard a group as the subject of History or to affirm the "absolute right" of the bourgeois of 1793, the bearer of the Revolution. We shall consider, in short, that an already lived History *resists* any a priori schematism. We shall understand that even this History, made and known—incident by incident—must be for us the object of a complete experience. We shall tax the contemporary Marxist with considering it to be the dead, transparent object of an immutable Knowledge.

We shall insist on the ambiguity of past facts; and by ambiguity, I do not mean—as Kierkegaard would—some sort of equivocal irrationality, but simply a contradiction which has never arrived at its point of maturity. It will be entirely proper to clarify the present by the future, the embryonic contradiction by the contradiction explicitly developed, and to leave to the present the equivocal aspects which it retains from its lived disparity.

Existentialism, then, can only affirm the specificity of the historical *event;* it seeks to restore to the event its function and its multiple dimensions. Of course, Marxists do not ignore the event; in their eyes it expresses the structure of society, the form which the class struggle has assumed, the relations of force, the ascending movement of the rising class, the contradictions which at the center of each class set particular groups with different interests in opposition to each other. But a Marxist aphorism shows how for almost a hundred years now, Marxists have tended not to attach much importance to the event. The outstanding event of the eighteenth century, they say, would not be the French Revolution but the appearance of the steam engine. Marx did not move in this direction, as is demonstrated very well by his excellent article *The Eighteenth Brumaire of Louis Napoleon Bonaparte.* But today the fact—like the person—tends to become more and more symbolic. The duty of the event is to verify the a priori analyses of the situation—or at least not to contradict them. Thus French Communists tend to describe facts in terms of what can-be or must-be. Here is how one of them—and not one of the least important—explains the Soviet intervention in Hungary.

Certain workers could be deceived, could commit themselves to a path which they did not believe to be that in which the counter-revolution was involving them, but subsequently these workers *could not help reflecting* on the consequences of this policy . . . [they] *could not do otherwise than be uneasy at seeing* [etc.]. . . . [They] could not (without indignation) see the return of the regent, Horthy. . . . It is *entirely natural* that under such circumstances the formation of the present Hungarian government has answered the prayers and expectation of the working class . . . in Hungary.

In this passage—the purpose of which is more political than theoretical—we are not told what the Hungarian workers did but what they *were unable not to do.* And why were they unable? Because they could not contradict their eternal essence as socialist workers. In a curious way, this Stalinized Marxism assumes an air of immobility; a worker is not a real being who changes with the world; he is a Platonic Idea. Indeed, in Plato, the Ideas are the Eternal, the Universal, the True. Motion and the event, as confused reflections of these static forms, are outside of Truth. Plato seeks to approach them through myths. In the Stalinist world the event is an edifying myth. Here we find what we might call the theoretical foundation for those fake confessions. The man who says, I have committed such and such an offense, such an act of treason, is performing a mythical, stereotyped recital, with no concern for verisimilitude, because he is asked to present his so-called crimes as the symbolic expression of an eternal essence. For example, the 1950 confession of abominable acts was for the purpose of unveiling the "true nature" of the Yugoslav regime. For us the most remarkable thing is the fact that the contradictions and errors in date, with which the confessions of Rajk were crammed full, never awakened in the Communists the vaguest suspicion. The materiality of fact is of no interest to these idealists; only its symbolic implications count in their eyes. In other words, Stalinist Marxists are blind to events. When they have reduced the meaning of them to the universal, they are quite willing to recognize that a residue remains, but they make of this residue the simple effect of chance. Fortuitous circumstances have been the occasional cause of what could not be dissolved (date, development, phases, origin and character of agents, ambiguity, misunderstandings, etc.). Thus, like individuals and particular enterprises, the lived falls over to the side of the irrational, the unutilizable, and the theoretician considers it to be *non-signifying*.

Existentialism reacts by affirming the specificity of the historical event, which it refuses to conceive of as the absurd juxtaposition of a contingent residue and an a priori signification. Its problem is to discover a supple, patient dialectic which espouses movements as they really are and which refuses to consider a priori that all lived conflicts pose contradictories or even contraries.[6] For us, *the interests* which come into play cannot necessarily find a mediation which reconciles them; most of the time they are mutually exclusive, but the fact that they cannot be satisfied at the same time does not necessarily prove that their reality is reduced to a pure contradiction of ideas. The thing stolen is not the contrary

[6] If two propositions are contradictory to each other, this means that one cannot be true without the other's being false, and vice versa (e.g., "A is true" and "A is not true"). If they are contrary, then they cannot both be true at once, but it is possible that both are false (e.g., "All S is P" and "No S is P"). H.B.

of the thief, nor is the exploited the contrary (or the contradictory) of the exploiter. Exploiter and exploited are men in conflict in a system whose principal characteristic is *scarcity*. To be sure, the capitalist owns the instruments of labor, and the worker does not own them: there we have a pure contradiction. But to be precise, this contradiction never succeeds in accounting for each event. It is the framework for the event; it creates a permanent tension in the social environment, a split within the capitalist society; but this fundamental structure of every contemporary event (in our bourgeois societies) does not by any means explain the event in its concrete reality. The day of the tenth of August, of the ninth of *Thermidor,* that day in the month of June 1848, etc., cannot be reduced to concepts. The relation between groups on each of those days is one of armed struggle, to be sure, and violence. But this struggle reflects *in itself* the structure of enemy groups, the immediate insufficiency of their development, the hidden conflicts which, though never clearly declared, result in an internal disequilibrium, the deviations which the present instruments impose on each one's action, the manner in which their needs and claims are manifested to each one.

Lefebvre has irrefutably established that after 1789, fear was the dominating passion of the revolutionary populace (which does not exclude heroism—quite the contrary) and that all these days of the popular offensive (July 14, June 20, August 10, September 3, etc.) are fundamentally *defensive* days. Military sections took the Tuileries by assault because they feared that an army of counter-revolutionaries might come forth from it some night to massacre Paris. *Today* this simple fact escapes Marxist analysis. The idealist voluntarism of the Stalinists can conceive only of an *offensive* action; it attributes negative sentiments to the class whose power is declining and to this class alone. Furthermore, when one recalls that the *sans-culottes,* mystified by the instruments of thought which they had at their disposal, allowed the immediate violence of their material needs to be transformed into an exclusively political violence, then one's idea of the Terror will be very different from the classical conception.

The event is not the passive resultant of a hesitant, distorted action and of an equally uncertain reaction; it is not even the fleeting, slippery synthesis of reciprocal incomprehensions. But across all the tools of action and thought which falsify *praxis,* each group realizes by its conduct a certain revelation of the other. Each of them is subject insofar as it directs its own action, and each is object insofar as it submits to the action of the other; each tactic foresees the other's tactic, more or less thwarts it, and is thwarted in turn. Inasmuch as each revealed activity of a group surpasses the activity of an opposing group, is modified in its tactics because of the latter and consequently modifies the structures of the group itself, the event in its full concrete reality is the organized unity of a plurality of oppositions reciprocally surpassed. Perpetually surpassed by the initiative of all and of each one, it surges up precisely from these very surpassings, as a double unified organization, the meaning of which is to realize in unity the destruction of each of its terms by the other. Thus constituted, the event reacts upon the men who compose it and imprisons them in its *apparatus;* of course, its being set up as an independent reality and its imposition on individuals are accomplished only by an immediate fetishizing. Already, for example, all the participants in the "day of August 10" know that the seizure of the Tuileries and the fall of the monarchy are at stake; the objective meaning of what they are doing is going to be imposed upon them as a real existence to the same degree that the other's resistance does not allow them to grasp their activity as the pure and simple objectification of themselves. Beginning here and precisely because the fetishizing has as a result the *realization* of fetishes, the event must be considered as a system in motion, drawing men along toward its own annihilation; the result is rarely clear-cut. On the evening of August 10, the King has not been deposed, but he is no longer at the Tuileries; he has been placed under the protection of the Assembly. His person remains just as embarrassing. The more real consequences of August 10 are, first, the appearance of the dual power (classical in Revolutions); second, the convocation of the Convention, which sets to work again at the basic problem, left unresolved by the event; finally, there is the dissatisfaction and growing unrest of the populace of Paris, which does not know whether or not its coup has succeeded. The result of this fear will be the September massacres. Thus it is the *very ambiguity* of the event which often confers upon it its historical efficacy. This is sufficient for us to affirm its specificity. For we do not wish to regard it as the simple unreal signification of molecular bumps and jolts—neither as their specific resultant nor as a schematic symbol of more profound movements. We view it rather as the moving, temporary unity of antagonistic groups which modifies them to the extent that they transform it.[7] As

[7] Obviously the conflict may be manifested here more or less clearly, or it may be veiled by the temporary complicity of the contending groups.

such, the event has its unique characteristics: its date, its speed, its structures, etc. The study of these factors allows us to make History rational even at the level of the concrete.

We must go further and consider in each case the role of the individual in the historic event. For this role is not defined once and for all: it is the structure of the groups considered which determines it in each case. Thereby, without entirely eliminating contingency, we restore to it its limits and its rationality. The group bestows its power and its efficacy upon the individuals whom it has made and who have made it in turn, whose irreducible particularity is one way of living universality. Through the individual the group looks back to itself and finds itself again in the particular opaqueness of life as well as in the universality of its struggle. Or rather, this universality takes on the face, the body, and the voice of the leaders whom it has given to itself; thus the event itself, while a collective apparatus, is more or less marked with individual signs; persons are reflected in it to the same extent that the conditions of the conflict and the structures of the group have permitted them to be personalized.

What we have said of the event is valid for the total history of the collectivity; this is what determines in each case and on each level the relations of the individual with society, his powers, and his efficacy. We willingly grant that Plekhanov is right in saying: "Influential personages can . . . modify the particular physiognomy of events and certain of their partial consequences, but they cannot change the orientation of the events." But that is not the question; the problem is to determine *on what level* we place ourselves in order to define reality.

Let us admit that another general, having risen to power, might have shown himself more conciliatory than Napoleon, might not have set all Europe against him, and would have died at the Tuileries and not at St. Helena. Then the Bourbons would not have returned to France. For them, of course, this result would have been the opposite of what actually happened. But in relation to the inner life of France as a whole, it would have been little different from the actual result. This "good soldier," after having re-established order and having assured the domination of the bourgeoisie, would not have delayed long before using pressure against it. . . . A liberal movement would then have been started . . . Louis-Philippe would perhaps have ascended the throne . . . in 1820 or in 1825. . . . But in any case the final outcome of the revolutionary movement would not have been contrary to what it was.

This passage, which has always made me laugh, I quote from the old-fashioned Plekhanov because I do not believe that Marxists have made any progress in this respect. There is no doubt that the final outcome would not have been different from what it was. But let us look at the variables which are eliminated: the bloody Napoleonic battles, the influence of revolutionary ideology on Europe, the occupation of France by the Allies, the return of the landowners, and the white Terror. Economically, as has been established today, the Restoration was a period of regression for France; the conflict between the property owners and the new bourgeoisie of the Empire delayed the development of the sciences and industry; the economic revival dates from 1830. One may admit that the advance of the bourgeoisie under a more peaceful emperor would not have been arrested and that France would not have kept that flavor of the *"Ancien Régime"* which so strongly impressed English visitors. As for the liberal movement, if it had come about at all, it would not have resembled the movement of 1830 in any way, since it would have lacked precisely the economic basis. Apart from all *that,* of course, the evolution would have been the same. Only, the "that," which is so disdainfully tossed over to the ranks of chance, is the whole life of men. Plekhanov, undismayed, looks on the terrible bloodshed of the Napoleonic wars, from which France was such a long time in recovering; he remains indifferent to the slowing up of economic and social life which marks the return of the Bourbons and from which the whole population had to suffer; he neglects the widespread misery which at about 1815 provoked the bourgeoisie into combat with religious fanaticism. As for the men who lived, suffered, and struggled under the Restoration and who ultimately got rid of the throne, no one of them would have been what he was or would have existed as such if Napoleon had not accomplished his *coup d'état.* What becomes of Hugo if his father is not a general of the Empire? And Musset? And Flaubert, who, as we have indicated, internalized the conflict between skepticism and faith? If after this we are told that these changes cannot modify the development of productive forces and the relations of production in the course of the last century, this is a truism. But if this development is to be made the sole object of human history, we simply fall back into the "economism" which we wanted to avoid; and Marxism becomes an "inhumanism."

Whatever men and events are, they certainly appear within the compass of *scarcity;* that is, in a society still incapable of emancipating itself from its needs— hence from nature—a society which is thereby defined according to its techniques and its tools. The split in a collectivity crushed by its needs and dominated by a mode of production raises up antagonisms among the individuals who compose it. The abstract relations of things with each other, of merchandise and money, etc., mask and condition the direct relations of men with one another. Thus machinery, the circulation of merchandise, etc., determine economic and social developments. Without these principles there is no historical rationality. But without living men, there is no history. The object of existentialism—due to the default of the Marxists—is the particular man in the social field, in his class, in an environment of collective objects and of other particular men. It is the individual, alienated, reified, mystified, as he has been made to be by the division of labor and by exploitation, but struggling against alienation with the help of distorting instruments and, despite everything, patiently gaining ground. The dialectical totalization must include acts, passions, work, and need as well as economic categories; it must at once place the agent or the event back into the historical setting, define him in relation to the orientation of becoming, and determine exactly the meaning of the present as such.

The Marxist method is progressive because it is the result—in the work of Marx himself—of long analyses. Today synthetic progression is dangerous. Lazy Marxists make use of it to constitute the real, a priori; political theorists use it to prove that what has happened had to happen just as it did. They can discover nothing by this method of pure *exposition*. The proof is the fact that they know in advance what they must find. Our method is heuristic; it teaches us something new because it is at once both regressive and progressive. Its first concern—as it is for the Marxist too—is to place man in his proper framework. We demand of general history that it restore to us the structures of the contemporary society, its conflicts, its profound contradictions, and the over-all movement which these determine. Thus we have at the outset a totalizing knowing of the moment considered, but in relation to the object of our study this knowing remains abstract. It begins with the material production of the immediate life and ends with the civil society, the State and the ideology. Now inside this movement our object is already *taking form,* and it is conditioned by these factors to the same degree that it conditions them. Thus its action is already inscribed in the totality considered, but it remains for us implicit and abstract. On the other hand, we have a certain partial acquaintance with our object; for example, we already know the biography of Robespierre insofar as it is a determination of temporality—that is, a succession of well-established facts. These facts appear concrete because they are known in detail, but they lack *reality,* since we cannot yet attach them to the totalizing movement.[8] This non-signifying objec-

---

[8] Saint-Just and Lebas, as soon as they arrived at Strasbourg, had the public accuser Schneider arrested "for his excesses." The fact is established. By itself it signifies nothing. Ought we to see in it the manifestation of revolutionary austerity (stemming from the reciprocity which, according to Robespierre, exists between Terror and Virtue)? This would be Ollivier's opinion. Or ought we to regard it as one of numerous examples of the authoritarian centralism of the petite bourgeoisie in power and as an effort on the part of the Committee of Public Safety to liquidate local authorities when they have *sprung from the people* and when they express too clearly the point of view of the *sans-culottes?* This is the interpretation offered by Daniel Guérin. According to which of these conclusions we choose (that is, from one or the other point of view on the *total* Revolution), the fact is radically transformed. Schneider becomes a tyrant or a martyr, his "excesses" appear as crimes or as pretexts. Thus the lived reality of the object brings with it all of its "depth"; that is, it is *at the same time*

tivity contains within itself, without being able to apprehend it, the entire period in which it has appeared— in the same way that the period, reconstituted by the historian, contains this objectivity. And yet our two pieces of abstract knowing fall outside one another. We know that the contemporary Marxist stops here. He claims to discover the object in the historical process and the historical process in the object. In actuality, he substitutes for both alike a collection of abstract considerations which immediately refer to principles. The existentialist method, on the contrary, wants to remain *heuristic*. It will have no other method than a continuous "cross-reference"; it will progressively determine a biography (for example) by examining the period, and the period by studying the biography. Far from seeking immediately to integrate one into the other, it will hold them separate until the reciprocal involvement comes to pass of itself and puts a temporary end to the research.

For any *given period*, we shall attempt to determine the field of possibles, the field of instruments, etc. If, for example, the problem is to discover the meaning of the historical action of Robespierre, we shall determine (among other things) the area of intellectual instruments. This will involve empty forms, the principal lines of force which appear in the concrete relations of contemporaries. Outside of precise acts of ideation, of writing, or of verbal designation, the Idea of Nature has no material being (still less an existence) in the eighteenth century. Yet it is real, for each individual takes it as something Other than his own specific act as

---

both maintained in its irreducibility and pierced through by a look which is going to seek, through it, all the structures which support it and ultimately the Revolution itself as a process of totalization.

reader or thinker insofar as it is also the thought of thousands of *other* thinkers. Thus the intellectual grasps his thought as being at once *his* and *other*. He thinks *in* the idea rather than the idea being *in* his thought; and this signifies that it is the sign of his belonging to a determined group (since its functions, ideology, etc., are known) and an undefined group (since the individual will never know all the members nor even the total number). As such, this "collective"—at once real and potential, real as a potentiality—represents a common instrument. The individual cannot avoid particularizing it by projecting himself through it toward his own objectification. It is therefore indispensable to define the living philosophy—as an unsurpassable horizon—and to give to these ideological schemata their true meaning. Indispensable also to study the intellectual attitudes of the period (*roles,* for example, many of which are also common instruments) by showing both their immediate theoretical meaning and their far-reaching efficacy (each potential idea, each intellectual attitude, appearing as an *enterprise* which is developed upon the ground of real conflicts and which must serve them). But we shall not judge their efficacy ahead of time as Lukacs and so many others do. We shall demand that the *comprehensive* study of schemata and roles release to us their real function—often manifold, contradictory, equivocal—without forgetting that the historical origin of the notion or of the attitude may have conferred upon it at the start another office, which remains inside these new functions as an outworn signification.

Bourgeois authors have used, for example, "the myth of the noble savage"; they have made of it a weapon against the nobility, but one would be oversimplifying the meaning and nature of this weapon if one forgot that it was invented by the Counter Reformation and used first against the Protestants' "bondage of the will." It is of primary importance in this connection not to pass over one fact which the Marxists systematically neglect—the *rupture* between the generations. From one generation to another an attitude, a schema, can close in upon itself, become a historical object, an example, a closed idea which would have to be re-opened or counterfeited from the outside. It would be necessary to know just *how* Robespierre's contemporaries received the Idea of Nature. (They had not contributed to its formation; they had got it, perhaps, from Rousseau, who was soon to die. It had a sacred character, due to the very fact of the *rupture*, that distance within proximity, etc.) The action and the life of the *Ancien Régime* (plutocracy is a worse regime), as well as the man whom we are to study, simply cannot be reduced to these abstract significations, to these impersonal attitudes. It is the man, on the contrary, who will give them force and life by the manner in which he will project himself by means of the Idea of Nature. We must therefore return to our object and study his personal statements (for example, Robespierre's speeches) through the screen of collective instruments.

The meaning of our study here must be a "differential," as Merleau-Ponty would call it. It is in fact the *difference* between the "Common Beliefs" and the concrete idea or attitude of the person studied, the way in which the beliefs are enriched, made concrete, deviated, etc., which, more than anything else, is going to enlighten us with respect to our object. This *difference* constitutes its uniqueness; to the degree that the individual utilizes "collectives," he depends—like all the members of his class or his milieu—upon a very general interpretation which already allows the regression to be pushed to material conditions. But to the degree that his behavior demands a differentiated interpretation, it will be necessary for us to form particular hypotheses within the abstract framework of universal significations. It is even possible that we may be led to reject the conventional schema for interpretation and to rank the object in a subgroup hitherto overlooked. This is the case with Sade, as we have seen. We are not at this point yet. What I want to indicate here is that we approach the study of the differential upon the basis of a totalizing demand. We do not regard these variations as anomic contingencies, as chances, as non-signifying aspects; quite the contrary, the singularity of the behavior or of the conception is *before all else* the concrete reality as a lived totalization. It is not a *trait* of the individual; it is the total individual, grasped in his process of objectification. The entire bourgeoisie of 1790 refers to *principles* when it envisions constructing a new State and providing it with a constitution. But the whole of Robespierre at that period is *in the particular way* in which he refers to the principles. I do not know of any good study of the "thought of Robespierre," and this is too bad. One would see that the universal in him is concrete (it is abstract in the other constituents) and that he merges with the idea of *totality*. The Revolution is a reality in process of totalization. False as soon as it stops—even more dangerous, if it is partial, than the aristocracy itself—it will be true when it has attained its full development. It is a totality in process of becoming which is to be realized one day as a totality which has become. The appeal to principles is then, with him, the sketching out of a dialectical genesis.

Like Robespierre himself, one would be deceived by instruments and by words if one believed (as he himself believed) that he *deduced* the consequences of his principles. The principles indicate a direction of the totalization. This is Robespierre *thinking:* a newborn dialectic which takes itself for an Aristotelian logic. But we do not believe that thought is a privileged determination. In the case of an intellectual or a political orator, we approach him in the first place because his thought is generally more easily accessible; it has been set down there in printed words. But the requirement for totalization requires that the individual be discovered whole in *all* his manifestations. Naturally this does not mean that there is no hierarchy among these. What we mean to say is that on whatever ground, at whatever level, one is considering him, the individual is always a whole. His vital behavior, his material conditioning, each is discovered as a particular opaqueness, as a finitude, and, at the same time, as a leaven in his most abstract thought; but reciprocally, at the level of his immediate life, his thought—contracted, implicit —exists already as the meaning of his behavior patterns. Robespierre's real mode of life (the frugality, economy, and modest dwelling of a petit bourgeois landlord and patriot), his clothing, his grooming, his refusal to use the familiar *tu*, his "incorruptibility," can give us their total meaning only when seen in the light of a certain political attitude which will be inspired by certain theoretical views (and which will in turn condition them). Thus the heuristic method must consider the "differential" (if the study of a person is concerned) within the perspective of biography.[9]

[9] This preliminary study is *indispensable* if we want to appraise Robespierre's role from 1793 until *Thermidor* 1794. It is not enough

What is involved, we see, is an analytic, regressive moment. Nothing can be discovered if we do not at the start proceed as far as is possible for us in the historical particularity of the object. I think now I ought to illustrate the regressive movement by a particular example.

Let us suppose that I wish to make a study of Flaubert—who is presented in histories of literature as the father of realism. I learn that he said: "I myself am Madame Bovary." I discover that his more subtle contemporaries—in particular Baudelaire, with his "feminine" temperament—had surmised this identification. I learn that the "father of realism" during his trip through the Orient dreamed of writing the story of a mystic virgin, living in the Netherlands, consumed by dreams, a woman who would have been the symbol of Flaubert's own cult of art. Finally, going back to his biography, I discover his dependence, his obedience, his "relative being," in short all the qualities which at that period were commonly called "feminine." At last I find out, a little late, that his physicians dubbed him a nervous old woman and that he felt vaguely flattered. Yet it is certain that he was *not to any degree at all* an invert.[1] Our problem then—without leaving the work itself; that is, the literary significations—is to ask

to show him supported and pushed forward by the movement of the Revolution; we must know also how he inscribed himself in it. Or, if you like, of what Revolution he is the epitome, the living condensation. It is this dialectic *alone* which will allow us to understand *Thermidor*. It is evident that we must not envision Robespierre as a certain *man* (a nature, a closed essence) determined by certain events, but that we must re-establish the open dialectic which goes from attitudes to events and vice versa without forgetting any of the original factors.

[1] His letters to Louise Colet show him to be narcissistic and onanist; but he boasts of amorous exploits, which must be true, since he is addressing the only person who can be both witness and judge of them.

ourselves why the author (that is, the pure synthetic activity which creates Madame Bovary) was able to metamorphose himself into a woman, what signification the metamorphosis possesses *in itself* (which presupposes a phenomenological study of Emma Bovary in the book), just what this woman is (of whom Baudelaire said that she possesses at once the folly and the will of a man), what the artistic transformation of male into female means in the nineteenth century (we must study the context of *Mlle de Maupin*, etc.), and finally, just who Gustave Flaubert *must have been* in order to have within the field of his possibles the possibility of portraying himself as a woman. The reply is independent of all biography, since this problem could be posed in Kantian terms: "Under what conditions is the feminization of experience possible?" In order to answer it, we must never forget that the author's style is directly bound up with a conception of the world; the sentence and paragraph structure, the use and position of the substantive, the verb, etc., the arrangement of the paragraphs, and the qualities of the narrative—to refer to only a few specific points—all express hidden presuppositions which can be determined *differentially* without as yet resorting to biography. Nevertheless, we shall never arrive at anything but *problems*. It is true that the statements of Flaubert's contemporaries will help us. Baudelaire asserted that the profound meaning of *The Temptation of St. Anthony*, a furiously "artistic" work which Bouilhet called "a diarrhea of pearls" and which in a completely confused fashion deals with the great metaphysical themes of the period (the destiny of man, life, death, God, religion, nothingness, etc.), is fundamentally identical with that of *Madame Bovary*, a work which is (on the surface) dry and objective. What kind of person, then, can Flaubert be, must he be, to express his own reality in the form of a frenzied idealism and of a realism more spiteful than detached? Who can he, must he, be in order to objectify himself in his work first as a mystic monk and then some years later as a resolute, "slightly masculine" woman?

At this point it is necessary to resort to biography—that is, to the facts *collected* by Flaubert's contemporaries and *verified* by historians. The work poses questions to the life. But we must understand in what sense; the work as the objectification of the person is, in fact, *more complete, more total* than the life. It has its roots in the life, to be sure; it illuminates the life, but it does not find its total explanation in the life alone. But it is too soon as yet for this total explanation to become apparent to us. The life is illuminated by the work as a reality whose total determination is found outside of it —both in the conditions which produce it and in the artistic creation which fulfills it and *completes it by expressing it.* Thus the work—when one has examined it—becomes a hypothesis and a research tool to clarify the biography. It questions and holds on to concrete episodes as replies to its questions.[2] But these answers

---

[2] I do not recall that anyone has been surprised that the Norman giant projected himself in his work as a woman. But I do not recall either that anyone has studied Flaubert's femininity (his truculent, "loud-mouthed" side has misled critics; but this is only a bit of camouflage, Flaubert has confirmed it a hundred times). Yet the order is discernible: the *logical scandal* is Madame Bovary, a masculine woman and feminized man, a lyric and realistic work. It is this scandal with its peculiar contradictions which must draw our attention to the life of Flaubert and to his lived femininity. We must detect it in his behavior—and first of all, in his sexual behavior. Now his letters to Louise Colet are sexual behavior; they are each one moments in the diplomacy of Flaubert with regard to this pertinacious poetess. We shall not find an embryonic *Madame Bovary* in the correspondence, but we shall greatly clarify the correspondence by means of Madame Bovary (and, of course, by the other works).

are not complete. They are insufficient and limited insofar as the objectification in art is irreducible to the objectification in everyday behavior. There is a hiatus between the work and the life. Nevertheless, the man, with his human relations thus clarified, appears to us in turn as a synthetic collection of questions. The work has revealed Flaubert's narcissism, his onanism, his idealism, his solitude, his dependence, his femininity, his passivity. But these qualities in turn are problems for us. They lead us to suspect at once both social structures (Flaubert is a property owner, he lives on unearned income, etc.) and a *unique* childhood drama. In short, these regressive questions provide us with the means to question his family group as a reality lived and denied by the child Flaubert. Our questions are based on two sorts of information: objective testimonies about the family (class characteristics, family type, individual aspect) and furiously subjective statements by Flaubert about his parents, his brother, his sister, etc. At this level we must be able constantly to refer back to the work and to know whether it contains a biographical truth such as the correspondence itself (falsified by its author) cannot contain. But we must know also that the work *never* reveals the secrets of the biography; the book can at most serve as a schema or conducting thread allowing us to discover the secrets in the life itself.

At this level, we study the early childhood as a way of living general conditions without clearly understanding or reflecting on them; consequently, we may find the meaning of the lived experience in the intellectual petite bourgeoisie, formed under the Empire, and in its way of living the evolution of French society. Here we pass over into the pure objective; that is, into the his-

torical totalization. It is History itself which we must
question—the halted advance of family capitalism, the
return of the landed proprietors, the contradictions in
the government, the misery of a still insufficiently developed Proletariat. But these interrogations are *constituting* in the sense in which the Kantian concepts are
called "constitutive"; for they permit us to realize concrete syntheses there where we had as yet only abstract,
general conditions. Beginning with an obscurely lived
childhood, we can reconstruct the true character of
petit bourgeois families. We compare Flaubert's with
the family of Baudelaire (at a more "elevated" social
level), with that of the Goncourt brothers (a petit bourgeois family which entered into the nobility about the
end of the eighteenth century by the simple acquisition
of "noble" property), with that of Louis Bouilhet, etc.
In this connection we study the real relations between
scientists and practitioners (the father Flaubert) and
industrialists (the father of his friend, Le Poittevin).
In this sense the study of the child Flaubert, as a universality lived in particularity, enriches the general
study of the petite bourgeoisie in 1830. By means of
the structures presiding over the particular family
group, we enrich and make concrete the always too
general characteristics of the class considered; in dis-
continuous "collectives," for example, we apprehend
the complex relation between a petite bourgeoisie of
civil servants and intellectuals, on the one hand, and
the "elite" of industrialists and landed proprietors on
the others, or, again, the *roots* of this petite bourgeoisie,
its peasant origin, etc., its relations with fallen aristo-
crats.[3] It is on this level that we are going to discover

[3] Flaubert's father, the son of a village veterinarian (a royalist),
"distinguished" by the imperial administration, marries a girl whose

the major contradiction which the child, Gustave Flaubert, lived in his own way: the opposition between the bourgeois analytic mind and the synthetic myths of religion. Here again a systematic cross-reference is established between the particular anecdotes which clarify these vague contradictions (because the stories gather them together into a single exploding whole) and the general determination of living conditions which allows us to reconstruct *progressively* (because they have already been studied) the material existence of the groups considered.

The sum total of these procedures—regression and cross-reference—has revealed what I shall call the profundity of the lived. Recently an essayist, thinking to refute existentialism, wrote: "It is not man who is profound; it is the world." He was perfectly right, and we agree with him without reservation. Only we should add that the world is human, the profundity of man is the world; therefore profundity comes to the world through man. The exploration of this profundity is a descent from the absolute concrete (*Madame Bovary* in the hands of a reader contemporary with Flaubert— whether it be Baudelaire or the Empress or the Prosecuting Attorney) to its most abstract conditioning (material conditions, the conflict of productive forces and of the relations of production insofar as these conditions appear in their universality and are given as lived by all the members of an undefined group [4]—that is, prac-

---

family is connected with the nobility through marriage. He associates with rich industrialists; he buys land.

[4] In reality the petite bourgeoisie in 1830 is a numerically defined group (although there obviously exist unclassifiable intermediaries who unite it with the peasant, the bourgeois, the landowners). But *methodologically* this concrete universal will always remain indeterminate because the statistics are incomplete.

tically, by *abstract* subjects). Across *Madame Bovary*
we can and must catch sight of the movement of landowners and capitalists, the evolution of the rising
classes, the slow maturation of the Proletariat: everything is there. But the most concrete significations are
radically irreducible to the most abstract significations.
The "differential" at each signifying plane reflects the
differential of the higher plane by impoverishing it and
by contracting it; it clarifies the differential of the lower
plane and serves as a rubric for the synthetic unification
of our most abstract knowing. This *cross-reference* contributes to enrich the object with all the profundity of
History; it determines, within the historical totalization, the still empty location for the object.

At this point in our research we have still not succeeded in revealing anything more than a hierarchy of
heterogeneous significations: *Madame Bovary*, Flaubert's "femininity," his childhood in a hospital building,
existing contradictions in the contemporary petite
bourgeoisie, the evolution of the family, of property,
etc.[5] Each signification clarifies the other, but their irreducibility creates a veritable discontinuity between
them. Each serves as an encompassing framework for
the preceding, but the included signification is richer
than the including signification. In a word, we have
only the outline for the dialectical movement, not the
movement itself.

It is then and only then that we must employ the pro-

[5] Flaubert's wealth consisted exclusively of real estate: this hereditary landlord will be ruined by industry; at the end of his life he will
sell his lands in order to save his son-in-law, who was involved in
foreign trade and had connections with Scandinavian industry. Mean-
while we shall see him often complaining that his rental income is
less than what the same investments would bring in if his father had
put it into industry.

gressive method. The problem is to recover the totalizing movement of enrichment which engenders each moment in terms of the prior moment, the impulse which starts from lived obscurities in order to arrive at the final objectification—in short, the *project* by which Flaubert, in order to escape from the petite bourgeoisie, will launch himself across the various fields of possibles toward the alienated objectification of himself and will constitute himself inevitably and indissolubly as the author of *Madame Bovary* and as that petit bourgeois which he refused to be. This project has *a meaning*, it is not the simple negativity of flight; by it a man aims at the production of himself in the world as a certain objective totality. It is not the pure and simple abstract decision to write which makes up the peculiar quality of Flaubert, but the decision to write in a certain manner in order to manifest himself in the world in a particular way; in a word, it is the particular signification—within the framework of the contemporary ideology—which he gives to literature as the negation of his original condition and as the objective solution to his contradictions. To rediscover the meaning of this "wrenching away from toward . . ." we shall be aided by our knowing all the signifying planes which he has traversed, which we have interpreted as his footprints, and which have brought him to the final objectification. We have the series: as we move back and forth between material and social conditioning and the work, the problem is to find the *tension* extending from objectivity to objectivity, to discover the law of expansion which surpasses one signification *by means of* the following one and which maintains the second in the first. In truth the problem is to invent a movement, to re-create it, but the hypothesis is immediately verifiable; the only valid one is that which will realize within a creative movement the transverse unity of *all* the heterogeneous structures.

Nevertheless, the project is in danger of being deviated, like Sade's project, by the collective instruments; thus the terminal objectification perhaps does not correspond exactly to the original choice. We must take up the regressive analysis again, making a still closer study of the instrumental field so as to determine the possible deviations; we must employ all that we have learned about the contemporary techniques of Knowledge as we look again at the unfolding life so as to examine the evolution of the choices and actions, their coherence or their apparent incoherence. *St. Anthony* expresses the whole Flaubert in his purity and in all the contradictions of his original project, but *St. Anthony* is a failure. Bouilhet and Maxime du Camp condemn it completely; they demand that it "tell a story." *There* is the deviation. Flaubert tells an anecdote, but he makes it support everything—the sky, hell, himself, St. Anthony, etc. The monstrous, splendid work which results from it, that in which he is objectified and alienated, is *Madame Bovary*. Thus the return to the biography shows us the hiatuses, the fissures, the accidents, at the same time that it confirms the hypothesis (the hypothesis of the original project) by revealing the direction and continuity of the life. We shall define the method of the existentialist approach as a regressive-progressive and analytic-synthetic method. It is at the same time an enriching cross-reference between the object (which contains the whole period as hierarchized significations) and the period (which contains the object in its totalization). In fact, when the object is *rediscovered* in its profundity and in its particularity, then instead of remaining external to the totalization (as it was up until the time when the Marxists undertook to integrate it into history), it enters immediately into contradiction with it. In short, the simple inert juxtaposition of the epoch and the object gives way abruptly to a living conflict.

If one has lazily defined Flaubert as a realist and if one has decided that realism suited the public in the Second Empire (which will permit us to develop a brilliant, completely false theory about the evolution of realism between 1857 and 1957), one will never succeed in comprehending either that strange monster which is *Madame Bovary* or the author or the public. Once more one will be playing with shadows. But if one has taken the trouble, in a study which is going to be long and difficult, to demonstrate within this novel the objectification of the subjective and its alienation—in short, if one grasps it in the concrete sense which it still holds at the moment when it escapes from its author and *at the same time* from the outside as an object which is allowed to develop freely, then the book abruptly comes to oppose the objective reality which it will hold for public opinion, for the magistrates, for contemporary writers. This is the moment to return to the period and to ask ourselves, for example, this very simple question: There was at that time a realist school —Courbet in painting and Duranty in literature were its representatives. Duranty had frequently presented his credo and drafted his manifestos. Flaubert despised realism and said so over and over throughout his life; he loved only the absolute purity of art. *Why* did the public decide at the outset that Flaubert was the realist, and why did it love in him *that particular realism;* that is, that admirable faked confession, that disguised lyricism, that implicit metaphysic? Why did it so value as an

admirable character portrayal of a woman (or as a piti-
less description of woman) what was at bottom only a
poor disguised man? Then we must ask ourselves *what
kind of realism* this public demanded or, if you prefer,
what kind of literature it demanded under that name
and why. This last moment is of primary importance; it
is quite simply the moment of alienation. Flaubert sees
his work stolen away from him by the very success
which the period bestows on it; he no longer recognizes
his book, it is foreign to him. Suddenly he loses his own
objective existence. But at the same time his work
throws a new light upon the period; it enables us to pose
a new question to History: Just what must that period
have been in order that it should demand *this* book and
mendaciously find there its own image. Here we are at
the veritable moment of historical action or of what I
shall willingly call the misunderstanding. But this is not
the place to develop this new point. It is enough to say
by way of conclusion that the man and his time will be
integrated into the dialectical totalization when we
have shown how History surpasses this contradiction.

· 3 ·

MAN defines himself by his project. This material being perpetually goes beyond the condition which is
made for him; he reveals and determines his situation
by transcending it in order to objectify himself—by
work, action, or gesture. The project must not be confused with the will, which is an abstract entity, although
the project can assume a voluntary form under certain
circumstances. This immediate relation with the Other
than oneself, beyond the given and constituted ele-

ments, this perpetual production of oneself by work and *praxis*, is our peculiar structure. It is neither a will nor a need nor a passion, but our needs—like our passions or like the most abstract of our thoughts—participate in this structure. They are always *outside of themselves toward . . .* This is what we call existence, and by this we do not mean a stable substance which rests in itself, but rather a perpetual disequilibrium, a wrenching away from itself with all its body. As this impulse toward objectification assumes various forms according to the individual, as it projects us across a field of possibilities, some of which we realize to the exclusion of others, we call it also choice or freedom. But it would be a mistake to accuse us of introducing the irrational here, of inventing a "first beginning" unconnected with the world, or of giving to man a freedom-fetish. This criticism, in fact, could only issue from a mechanist philosophy; those who would direct it at us do so because they would like to *reduce praxis,* creation, invention, to the simple reproduction of the elementary given of our life. It is because they would like to *explain* the work, the act, or the attitude by the factors which condition it; their desire for explanation is a disguise for the wish to assimilate the complex to the simple, to deny the specificity of structures, and to reduce change to identity. This is to fall back again to the level of scientistic determinism. The dialectical method, on the contrary, refuses to *reduce;* it follows the reverse procedure. It surpasses by conserving, but the terms of the surpassed contradiction cannot account for either the transcending itself or the subsequent synthesis; on the contrary, it is the synthesis which clarifies them and which enables us to understand them. For us the basic contradiction is only one of the factors which delimit and structure the field of possibles; it is the choice which must be interrogated if one wants to explain them in their detail, to reveal their singularity (that is, the particular aspect in which *in this case* generality is presented), and to understand how they have been lived. It is the work or the act of the individual which reveals to us the secret of his conditioning. Flaubert by his choice of writing discloses to us the meaning of his childish fear of death—not the reverse. By misunderstanding these principles, contemporary Marxism has prevented itself from understanding significations and values. For it is as absurd to reduce the signification of an object to the pure inert materiality of that object itself as to want to deduce the law from the fact. The meaning of a conduct and its value can be grasped only in perspective by the movement which realizes the possibles as it reveals the given.

Man is, for himself and for others, a signifying being, since one can never understand the slightest of his gestures without going beyond the pure present and explaining it by the future. Furthermore, he is a creator of signs to the degree that—always ahead of himself—he employs certain objects to designate other absent or future objects. But both operations are reduced to a pure and simple surpassing. To surpass present conditions toward their later change and to surpass the present object toward an absence are one and the same thing. Man constructs signs because in his very reality he is signifying; and he is signifying because he is a dialectical surpassing of all that is simply given. What we call freedom is the irreducibility of the cultural order to the natural order.

To grasp the meaning of any human conduct, it is necessary to have at our disposal what German psychiatrists and historians have called "comprehension." But what is involved here is neither a particular talent nor a special faculty of intuition; this knowing is simply the dialectical movement which explains the act by its terminal signification in terms of its starting conditions. It is originally progressive. If my companion suddenly starts toward the window, I understand his gesture in terms of the material situation in which we both are. It is, for example, because the room is too warm. He is going "to let in some air." This action is not inscribed in the temperature; it is not "set in motion" by the warmth as by a "stimulus" provoking chain reactions. There is present here a synthetic conduct which, by unifying itself, unifies before my eyes the practical field in which we both are. The movements are new, they are adapted to the situation, to particular obstacles. This is because the perceived settings are *abstract* motivating schemata and insufficiently determined; they are determined within the unity of the enterprise. It is necessary to avoid that table; after that the window is of the casement type or a sash window or a sliding one or perhaps—if we are in a strange place—of a style not yet known to us. In every way, if I am to go beyond the succession of gestures and to perceive the unity which they give themselves, I must myself feel the overheated atmosphere as a need for freshness, as a demand for air; that is, I must myself become the lived surpassing of our material situation. Within the room, doors and windows are never entirely passive realities; the work of other people has given to them their meaning, has made out of them instruments, possibilities *for an other* (any other). This means that I *comprehend* them already as instrumental structures and as products of a directed activity. But my companion's movement makes explicit the crystallized indications and designations in these products; his behavior reveals the practical field to me as a "hodological space," and conversely the indications contained in the utensils become the crystallized meaning which allows me to comprehend the enterprise. His conduct *unifies* the room, and the room defines his conduct.

What we have here is so clearly an enriching surpassing *for both of us* that this conduct, instead of being first clarified by the material situation, can reveal the situation to me. Absorbed in the collaborating work of our discussion, I had experienced the warmth as a confused, unnamed discomfort; in my companion's gesture, I see at once both his practical intention and the meaning of my discomfort. The movement of comprehension is simultaneously progressive (toward the objective result) and regressive (I go back toward the original condition). Moreover, it is the act itself which will define the heat as unbearable; if we don't lift a finger, it is because the temperature can be tolerated. Thus the rich, complex unity of the enterprise springs from the poorest condition and turns back upon it to clarify it. Furthermore, at the same time but in another dimension, my companion reveals himself by his conduct. If he gets up deliberately and opens the window a crack before beginning the work or the discussion, this gesture refers to more general objectives (the will to show himself methodical, to play the role of an orderly man, or his real love of order). He will appear very different if he suddenly jumps to his feet and throws the casement window wide open as if he were suffocating. Here also if I am to be able to comprehend him, it is necessary that my own conduct in its projective movement should inform me about my own inner depths—that is, about my wider objectives and the conditions which correspond to the choice of these objectives. Thus *comprehension* is nothing other than my real life; it is the totalizing movement which gathers together my neighbor, myself, and the environment in the synthetic unity of an objectification in process.

Precisely because we are a *pro-ject,* comprehension may be entirely regressive. If neither one of us has been aware of the temperature, a third person coming in will certainly say: "Their discussion is so absorbing that they are about to stifle." This person, from the minute he entered the room, has lived the warmth as a need, as a wish to let in some air, to freshen things up; suddenly the closed window has assumed for him a signification, not because it was going to be opened, but, quite the contrary, because it had not been opened. The close, overheated room reveals to him an act which has not been performed (and which was indicated as a permanent possibility by the work laid down in the present utensils). But this absence, this objectification of nonbeing, will find a true consistency only if it serves to reveal a positive enterprise. Across the act to be done and not yet done, this witness will discover the passion which we have put into our discussion. And if he laughingly calls us "library rats," he will find still more general significations in our behavior and will illuminate us to the depths of our being.

Because we are men and because we live in the world of men, of work, and of conflicts, all the objects which surround us are signs. By themselves they indicate their use and scarcely mask the real project of those who have made them such *for us* and who address us through them. But their particular ordering, under this or that circumstance, retraces for us an individual action, a project, an event. The cinema has so often used this process that it has become a convention. The director shows us the beginning of a dinner, then he cuts; several hours later in the deserted room, overturned glasses, empty bottles, cigarette stubs littering the floor, indicate by themselves that the guests got drunk. Thus significations come from man and from his project, but they are inscribed everywhere in things and in the order of things. Everything at every instant is always signifying, and significations reveal to us men and relations among men across the structures of our society. But these significations appear to us only insofar as we ourselves are signifying. Our comprehension of the Other is never contemplative; it is only a moment of our *praxis,* a way of living—in struggle or in complicity—the concrete, human relation which unites us to him.

Among these significations there are some which refer us to a lived situation, to specific behavior, to a collective event. This would be the case, if you like, with those shattered glasses which, on the screen, are charged with retracing for us the story of an evening's orgy. Others are simple indications—such as an arrow on the wall in a subway corridor. Some refer to "collectives." Some are symbols; the reality signified is present in them as the nation is in the flag. Some are statements of utility; certain objects are offered to me as *means*—a pedestrian crossing, a shelter, etc. Still others, which we apprehend especially—but not always—by means of the visible, immediate behavior of real men, are quite simply ends.

We must resolutely reject the so-called "positivism" which imbues today's Marxist and impels him to deny the existence of these last significations. The supreme mystification of positivism is that it claims to approach social experience without any a priori whereas it has decided at the start to deny one of its fundamental structures and to replace it by its opposite. It was legitimate for the natural sciences to free themselves from the anthropomorphism which consists in bestowing human properties on inanimate objects. But it is perfectly absurd to assume by analogy the same scorn for anthropomorphism where anthropology is concerned. When one is studying man, what can be more exact or more rigorous than to *recognize human properties in him?* The simple inspection of the social field ought to have led to the discovery that the relation to ends is a permanent structure of human enterprises and that it is *on the basis of this relation* that real men evaluate actions, institutions, or economic constructions. It ought to have been established that our comprehension of the other is necessarily attained through ends. A person who from a distance watches a man at work and says: "I don't understand what he is doing," will find that clarification comes when he can unify the disjointed moments of this activity, thanks to the anticipation of the result aimed at. A better example—in order to fight, to outwit the opponent, a person must have at his disposal several systems of ends at once. In boxing, one will grant to a feint its true finality (which is, for example, to force the opponent to lift his guard) if one discovers and rejects at the same time its pretended finality (to land a left hook on the forehead). The double, triple systems of ends which others employ condition our activity as strictly as our own. A positivist who held on to his teleological color blindness in practical life would not live very long.

It is true that in a society which is wholly alienated, in which "capital appears more and more as a social power of which the capitalist is the functionary," [6] the manifest ends can mask the profound necessity behind an evolution or a mechanism already set. But even then the end as the signification of the lived project of a man or of a group of men remains real, to the extent that, as Hegel said, the appearance possesses a reality as appearance. In this case as well as in the preceding, its role and its practical efficacy must be determined. In *Critique of Dialectical Reason* I shall show how the stabilization of prices in a competitive market *reifies* the relation between seller and buyer. Courtesies, hesitations, bargaining, all that is outmoded and thrust aside, since the chips are already down. And yet each of these *gestures* is lived by its author as an act. Of course, this activity does not belong to the domain of pure representation. But the permanent possibility that an end might be transformed into an illusion characterizes the social field and the modes of alienation; it does not remove from the end its irreducible structure. Still better, the notions of alienation and mystification have meaning only to the precise degree that they steal away the ends and disqualify them. There are therefore two conceptions which we must be careful not to confuse. The first, which is held by numerous American sociologists and by some French Marxists, foolishly substitutes for the givens of experience an abstract causalism or certain metaphysical forms or concepts such as motivation, attitude, or role, which have no meaning except in conjunction with a finality. The second recognizes the existence of ends wherever they are found and limits itself to declaring that certain among them can be neutralized at the heart of the historical process

---

[6] Marx: *Capital*, III, 1, p. 293.

of totalization.[7] This is the position of true Marxism and of existentialism.

The dialectical movement, which proceeds from the objective conditioning to objectification, enables us to understand that the ends of human activity are not mysterious entities added on to the act itself; they represent simply the surpassing and the maintaining of the given in an act which goes from the present toward the future. The end is the objectification itself inasmuch as it constitutes the dialectical law of a human conduct and the unity of its internal contradictions. The presence of the future at the heart of the present will not be surprising if one stops to consider that the end is enriched at the same time as the action itself; it surpasses this action inasmuch as it makes the unity of the action, but the content of this unity is never more concrete nor more explicit than the unified enterprise is at the same instant. From December 1851 until April 30, 1856, *Madame Bovary* made the real unity of all Flaubert's actions. But this does not mean that the precise, concrete work, with all its chapters and all its sentences, was figuring at the heart of the writer's life in 1851—even as an enormous absence. The end is transformed, it passes from the abstract to the concrete, from the global to the detailed. At each moment it is the actual unity of the operation or, if you prefer, the unification of the means

[7] The contradiction between the reality of an end and its objective nonexistence appears every day. To cite only the commonplace example of a fight—the boxer who, deceived by a feint, lifts his guard to protect his eyes, is really pursuing an end; but for his opponent, who wants to punch him in the stomach, this end—in itself or objectively—becomes the *means* for carrying through the punch. By making himself a subject, the maladroit boxer has realized himself as an object. His end has become the accomplice of his opponent's. It is end and means at once. We shall see in *Critique of Dialectical Reason* that the "atomization of crowds" and recurrence both contribute to turning ends back against those who posit them.

in action. Always *on the other side of the present*, it is fundamentally only *the present itself seen from its other side*. Yet in its structures it holds relations with a more distant future. Flaubert's immediate objective, to conclude *this* paragraph, is itself clarified by the distant objective which sums up the whole operation—to produce *this* book. But as the desired result is more of a totalization, it becomes that much more abstract. At first Flaubert writes to his friends: "I would like to write a book which would be . . . like this . . . like that. . . ." The obscure sentences which he uses at this stage have more meaning for the author than they have for us, but they give neither the structure nor the real content of the work. Still they will not cease to serve as a framework for all the later creative work, for the plot, for the choice of characters. "The book which must be . . . this and that" is also *Madame Bovary*. Then, too, in the case of a writer the immediate end of his present work is clarified only in relation to a hierarchy of future significations (that is, of ends), each one of which serves as a framework for the preceding and as content for the following. The end is enriched in the course of the enterprise; it develops and surpasses its contradictions along with the enterprise itself. When the objectification is terminated, the concrete richness of the object produced infinitely surpasses that of the end (taken as a unitary hierarchy of meanings) at any moment of the past at which it is considered. But this is precisely because the object is no longer an end; it is the product "in person" of labor, and it exists in the world, which implies an infinity of new relations (the relation of its elements, one with the other, within the new objective milieu, its own relation with other cultural objects, the relation between itself as a cultural product and men).

Such as it is in its reality as an objective product, it necessarily refers back to an elapsed, now vanished operation for which it has served as end. And if in the course of reading the book, we do not constantly go back (albeit vaguely and abstractly) to the desires and ends —that is, to the total enterprise—of Flaubert, we simply make a fetish out of the book (which often happens) just as one may do with a piece of merchandise by considering it as a thing that speaks for itself and not as the reality of a man objectified through his work. For the comprehensive regression of the reader, the order is exactly the reverse. The totalizing concrete is the book; the author's life and the enterprise of writing it, like a dead past which is far removed, spread out in a series of significations extending from the richest to the poorest, from the most concrete to the most abstract, from the most particular to the most general, and these in turn refer us from the subjective to the objective.

If we refuse to see the original dialectical movement in the individual and in his enterprise of producing his life, of objectifying himself, then we shall have to give up dialectic or else make of it the immanent law of History. We have seen both these extremes. Sometimes in the work of Engels, dialectic explodes, men bump against each other like physical molecules, the resultant of all these opposing agitations is *a statistical mean*. But a mean result cannot by itself alone become an apparatus or a process. It is registered passively, it does not impose itself, whereas capital, "an alienated, autonomous social power, as an object, and as the power of the capitalist, *is opposed* to society by the intervention of this object." [8] To avoid the mean result and the Stalinist statistical fetishism, non-Communist

[8] *Capital*, III, 1, p. 293.

Marxists have preferred to dissolve the concrete man in synthetic objects, to study the contradictions and movements of collectives as such. They have gained nothing by this; finality takes refuge in the concepts which they borrow or forge. Bureaucracy becomes a person with his enterprises, his projects, etc.; he has attacked the Hungarian democracy (another person) because he could not tolerate . . . and with the intention of . . . etc. They escape from scientist determinism only to fall into absolute idealism.

In truth, the passage from Marx shows that he admirably understood the problem. Capital is opposed to society, he said. And yet it is a social power. The contradiction is explained by the fact that capital has become an *object*. But this object, which is not "a social mean," but, on the contrary, an "antisocial reality," is maintained as such only to the extent that it is sustained and directed by the real and active power of the *capitalist* (who is in turn entirely possessed by the alienated objectification of his own power; for his power becomes the object of other surpassings by other capitalists). These relations are molecular because *there are only* individuals and particular relations among them (opposition, alliance, dependence, etc.); but they are not mechanical, because *in no case* are we dealing with the colliding of simple inertias. Within the unity of his own enterprise, each person surpasses the other and incorporates him as a means (and vice versa); each pair of unifying relations is in turn surpassed by the enterprise of a third. Thus at each level there are constituted hierarchies of enveloping and enveloped ends, where the former steal the signification from the latter and the latter aim at shattering the former. Each time that the enterprise of a man or of a group of men becomes an ob-

ject for other men who surpass it toward their ends and
for the whole of society, this enterprise guards its finality as its real unity, and it becomes, for the very people who initiated it, an external object which tends to
dominate them and to survive them. (In *Critique of
Dialectical Reason* we shall see certain general conditions for this alienation.) Thus are constituted systems,
apparatus, instruments, which are real objects possess-
ing material bases in existence; at the same time they
are *processes* pursuing—within society and often
against them—ends which no longer belong to any-
body but which, as the alienating objectification of ends
really pursued, become the objective, totalizing unity of
collective objects. The process of capital offers this rigor
and this necessity only in a perspective that makes of it,
not a social structure or a regime, but a material *apparatus,* whose relentless movement is the reverse side of
an infinity of unifying *surpassings.* Therefore, for a
given society, the correct procedure will be to take into
account both the living ends which correspond to the
particular effort of a person, of a group, or of a class and
also the impersonal finalities, the by-products of our activity which derive their unity from it and which ultimately become the essential, imposing their structures
and their laws on all our enterprises.[9] The social field

---

[9] The Black Death brought about an increase in the wages of farm
workers in England. Thereby it obtained what only a concerted action
on the part of the peasants could otherwise have obtained (and such
action was inconceivable during that period). What is the source of
this *human* efficacy in the pestilence? It is the fact that its place, its
scope, its victims, were determined ahead of time by the government;
the landowners took shelter in their castles; the crowding together of
the common people is the perfect environment for the spreading of
the disease. The Black Death acts only as an *exaggeration* of the class
relations; it *chooses.* It strikes the wretched, it spares the wealthy. But
the result of this reversed finality is the same as what the anarchists
wanted to achieve (when they counted on economic Malthusianism

is full of acts with no author, of constructions without constructor. If we rediscover in man his veritable humanity—that is, the power to make History by pursuing his own ends—*then* in a period of alienation we shall see that the non-human is presented with all the appearances of the human and that the "collectives," perspectives of flight across men, retain in themselves the finality which characterizes human relations.

This does not mean, of course, that everything is either a personal finality or an impersonal one. Material conditions impose their factual necessity. *The fact is* that there is no coal in Italy. All the industrial evolution of this country in the nineteenth and twentieth centuries depends on this irreducible given. But as Marx has often insisted, the geographical givens (or any other kind) can act only within the compass of a given society, in conformity with its structures, its economic regime, the institutions which it has given itself. What does this mean if not that the necessity of fact can be grasped only by means of human constructions? The indissoluble unity of these "apparatus," these monstrous constructions with no author, in which man loses himself and which forever escape him, with their rigorous functioning, their reversed finality (which should be called, I think, a *counter-finality*), with their pure or "natural" necessities and the furious struggle of alienated men—this indissoluble unity must appear to every inquirer who wants to comprehend the social world. These objects are there before our eyes. But before showing their substructural conditioning, our inquirer

---

to force an increase in wages). The scarcity of manual laborers—a synthetic, collective result—compels the financial barons to pay higher. The population was quite right to personify this affliction and to call it "the Black Death." But its unity reflects in reverse the split unity of English society.

must see them as they are, without neglecting any of their structures. For he will be obliged to account for everything, for the necessity and the finality which are so strangely intermingled. He will have to disengage the counter-finalities which dominate us and at the same time show the more or less concerted enterprises which exploit them or oppose them. He will take the given as it manifests itself, with its visible ends, before he even knows whether these ends express the intention of any real person. The more easily he has at his disposal a philosophy, a point of view, a theoretical basis of interpretation and totalization, the more he will force himself to approach these ends in a spirit of absolute empiricism; he will allow them to develop, to release by themselves their immediate meaning, for he will have the intention of *learning*, not *rediscovering*. It is in this free development that we find the conditions and the first outline of the object's *situation* in relation to the social whole and its totalization inside the historical process.[1]

[1] In a certain philosophy today, it is the fashion to reserve the function of *signifying* for institutions (taken in the broadest sense) and to reduce the individual (save in exceptional cases) or the concrete group to the role of the *signified*. This view is true to the extent that, for example, the colonel in uniform who goes into the barracks is *signified* in his function and in his rank by his clothing and by his distinctive insignia. In fact I perceive the sign before the man; I see *a* colonel crossing the street. This is true again insofar as the colonel enters *into his role* and displays himself to his subordinates by the rituals and mimicry which signify authority. Ritual and mimicry are learned; they are significations which he does not produce by himself and which he is limited to reconstructing. These considerations may be extended to civil dress, to one's deportment. Clothing bought at the Galeries Lafayette is by itself a signification. And of course what is signified is the period, the social condition, the nationality, and the age of the buyer. But we must never forget—under pain of giving up all dialectical comprehension of the social—that the reverse is also true; the majority of these objective significations, which seem to exist all alone and which are put upon particular men, are also created by

men. And the men themselves, who put them on and present them to others, can appear as signified *only by making themselves signifying;* that is, by trying to objectify themselves *through* the attitudes and the roles which society imposes upon them. Here again men *make history* on the basis of prior conditions. All the significations are recovered and surpassed by the individual as he moves toward inscribing in things his own *total* signification. The colonel makes himself a signified colonel only in order to be himself signified (that is, a totality which he considers more complex). The Hegel-Kierkegaard conflict finds its solution in the fact that man is neither signified nor signifying but *at once* (like Hegel's absolute-subject but in a different sense) both the signified-signifying and the signifying-signified.

◉◉◉◉◉◉◉◉◉◉◉◉◉◉◉◉◉◉◉◉◉◉◉◉◉◉◉

CONCLUSION

SINCE Kierkegaard, a certain number of ideologists, in their attempt to distinguish between being (*être*) and knowing (*savoir*), have succeeded in describing better what we might call "the ontological region" of existences. Without prejudice to the givens of animal psychology and psychobiology, it is evident that the *presence-in-the-world* described by these ideologists characterizes a sector—or perhaps even the whole—of the animal world. But within this living universe, man occupies, *for us,* a privileged place. First, because he is able to be historical; [1] that is, he can continually define himself by his own *praxis* by means of changes suffered or provoked and their internalization, and then by the very surpassing of the internalized relations. Second, because he is characterized as *the existent which*

---

[1] Man should not be defined by historicity—since there are some societies without history—but by the permanent possibility of living *historically* the breakdowns which sometimes overthrow societies of repetition. This definition is necessarily a posteriori; that is, it arises at the heart of a historical society, and it is in itself the result of social transformations. But it goes back to apply itself to societies without history in the same way that history itself returns to them to transform them—first externally and then in and through the internalization of the external.

we are. In this case the questioner finds himself to be precisely the questioned, or, if you prefer, human reality is the existent whose being is in question in its being. It is evident that this "being-in-question" must be taken as a determination of *praxis* and that the theoretical questioning comes in only as an abstract moment of the total process. Moreover, knowing is inevitably practical; it changes the known. Not in the sense of classical rationalism. But in the way that an experiment in microphysics necessarily transforms its object.

In choosing as the object of our study, within the ontological sphere, that privileged existent which is man (privileged *for us*), it is evident that existentialism poses to itself the question of its fundamental relations with those disciplines which are grouped under the general heading of *anthropology*. And—although its field of application is theoretically larger—existentialism is anthropology too insofar as anthropology seeks to give itself a foundation. Let us note, in fact, that the problem is the same one which Husserl defined apropos of sciences in general: classical mechanics, for example, *uses* space and time as being each one a homogeneous and continuous milieu, but it never *questions* itself about time or space or motion. In the same way, the sciences of man *do not question themselves* about man; they study the development and the relation of human facts, and man appears as a signifying milieu (determinable by significations) in which particular facts are constituted (such as the structures of a society or a group, the evolution of institutions, etc.). Thus if we take it for granted that experience will give us the complete collection of facts concerning any group whatsoever and that the anthropological disciplines will bind together these facts by means of objective, strictly defined relations, then "human reality" as such will be no more accessible for us than the space of geometry or mechanics—for this fundamental reason, that our research is not aimed at revealing but at constituting laws and at bringing to light functional relations or processes.

But to the degree that anthropology at a certain point in its development perceives that it is denying man (by the systematic rejection of anthropomorphism) or that it takes him for granted (as the ethnologist does at every moment), it implicitly demands to know what is the *being* of human reality. Between an ethnologist or a sociologist—for whom history is too often only the movement which disarranges the lines of division—and a historian—for whom the very permanence of structures is a perpetual change—the essential difference and opposition are derived much less from the diversity of methods [2] than from a more profound contradiction which touches on the very meaning of human reality. If anthropology is to be an organized whole, it must surmount this contradiction—the origin of which does not reside in a Knowledge but in reality itself—and it must on its own constitute itself as a structural, historical anthropology.

This task of integration would be easy if one could bring to light some sort of *human essence;* that is, a fixed collection of determinations in terms of which one could assign a definite place to the objects studied. But the majority of anthropologists agree that the diversity of groups—considered from the synchronic point of view—and the diachronic evolution of societies forbid us to found anthropology upon a conceptual knowledge. It would be impossible to find a "human nature" which

[2] In a rational anthropology they could be co-ordinated and integrated.

is common to the Murians, for example, and to the historical man of our contemporary societies. But, conversely, a real communication and in certain situations a reciprocal comprehension are established or can be established between existents thus distinct (for example, between the ethnologist and the young Murians who speak of their *gothul.*) It is in order to take into account these two opposed characteristics (no common *nature* but an always possible communication) that the movement of anthropology once again and in a new form gives rise to the "ideology" of existence.

This ideology, in fact, considers that human reality eludes direct knowledge to the degree that it *makes itself.* The determinations of the person appear only in a society which constantly constructs itself by assigning to each of its members a specific work, a relation to the product of his work, and relations of production with the other members—all of this in a never-ceasing movement of totalization. But these determinations are themselves sustained, internalized, and lived (whether in acceptance or refusal) by a *personal project* which has two fundamental characteristics: first, it cannot under any circumstances be defined by concepts; second, as a *human* project it is always *comprehensible* (theoretically if not actually). To make this comprehension *explicit* does not by any means lead us to discover abstract notions, the combination of which could put the comprehension back into conceptual Knowledge; rather it reproduces the dialectic movement which starts from simply existing givens and is raised to signifying activity. This comprehension, which is not distinguished from *praxis,* is at once both immediate existence (since it is produced as the movement of action) and the foundation of an indirect knowing of existence (since it comprehends the ex-istence of the other).

By indirect knowing we mean the result of reflection on existence. This knowing is indirect in this sense—that it is presupposed by all the concepts of anthropology, whatever they may be, without being itself made the object of concepts. Whatever the discipline considered, its most elementary notions would be *incomprehensible* without the *immediate comprehension* of the *project* which underlies them, of negativity as the basis of the project, of transcendence as the existence outside-of-itself in relation with the Other-than-itself and the Other-than-man, of the surpassing as a mediation between the given that is simply there and the practical signification, of *need,* finally, as the being-outside-of-itself-in-the-world on the part of a practical organism.[3] It is useless to try to disguise this comprehension of the project by a mechanistic positivism, a materialist "Gestaltism." It remains, and it supports the discussion. The dialectic itself—which could not be made the object of concepts because its movement engenders and dissolves them all—appears as History and as historical Reason only upon the foundation of existence; for it is the development of *praxis,* and *praxis* is inconceivable without *need, transcendence,* and the *project.* The very employment of these vocables to designate existence in the structures of its unveiling indicate to us that it is capable of *denotation.* But the relation of the sign or signi-

---

[3] There is no question of denying the fundamental priority of need; on the contrary, we mention it last to indicate that it sums up in itself all the existential structures. In its full development, need is a transcendence and a negativity (negation of negation inasmuch as it is produced as a lack seeking to be denied), hence a *surpassing-toward* (a rudimentary pro-ject).

fied cannot be conceived of here in the form of an empirical signification. The signifying movement—inasmuch as language is at once an immediate attitude of each person in relation to all and a human product—is itself a project. This means that the existential project will be in the word which will denote it, not as the signified—which on principle is *outside*—but as its original foundation and its very structure. And of course the very word "language" has a conceptual signification; one part of the language can designate the whole conceptually. But the language is not in the word as the reality providing the basis for all nomination; the contrary is true, and every word is the whole language. The word "project" originally designates a certain human attitude (one "makes" projects) which supposes as its foundation the pro-ject, an existential structure. And this word, as a word, is possible only as a particular effectuation of human reality inasmuch as it is a pro-ject. In this sense the word by itself manifests the project from which it derives only in the way in which the piece of merchandise retains in itself and passes on to us the human work which has produced it.[4]

Yet what is involved is an entirely rational process. In fact the word, although it regressively designates its act, refers to the fundamental comprehension of human reality in each one and in all. This comprehension, always actual, is given in all *praxis* (individual or collective) although not in systematic form. Thus words—even those which do not try to refer regressively to the fundamental, dialectical act—contain a regressive indication referring to the comprehension of that act. And those which try to unveil the existential structures ex-

[4] In our society this must first take the form of fetishizing the word.

plicitly, are limited to denoting regressively the reflective act inasmuch as it is a structure of existence and a practical operation which existence performs upon itself. The original irrationalism of the Kierkegaardian attempt disappears entirely to give place to anti-intellectualism. The concept, indeed, aims at the object (whether this object be outside man or in him), and precisely for this reason, it is an intellectual *Knowledge*.[5] In language, man designates himself insofar as he is the object of man. But in the effort to recover the source of every sign and consequently of all objectivity, language turns back upon itself to indicate the moments of a comprehension forever in process, since it is nothing other than existence itself. In giving names to these moments, one does not transform them into *Knowledge*—since this concerns the internal, and what we shall in *Critique of Dialectical Reason*, call the "pratico-inerte."[6] But one stakes out the comprehensive actualization by means of indications which refer simultaneously to reflective practice and to the content of comprehensive reflection. Need, negativity, surpassing, project, transcendence, form a synthetic totality in which each one of the moments designated contains all the others. Thus the reflective operation—as a particular, dated act—can be indefinitely repeated. Thereby the dialectic develops indefinitely and wholly in each

---

[5] It would be an error to believe that comprehension refers to the *subjective*. For *subjective* and *objective* are two opposed and complementary characteristics of man *as an object of knowledge*. In fact, the question concerns action itself *qua action;* that is, distinct on principle from the results (objective and subjective) which it engenders.

[6] This is Sartre's own term. He uses it to refer to the external world, including both the material environment and human structures—the formal rules of a language, public opinion as expressed and molded by news media, any "worked-over matter" which modifies my conduct by the mere fact of its being there. H.B.

dialectic process, whether it be individual or collective.

But this reflective operation would not need to be repeated and would be transformed into a formal knowledge if its content could exist by itself and be separated
from concrete, historical actions, strictly defined by the
situation. The true role of the "ideologies of existence"
is not to describe an abstract "human reality" which has
never existed, but constantly to remind anthropology of
the existential dimension of the processes studied. Anthropology studies only objects. Now man is the being
by whom becoming-an-object comes to man. Anthropology will deserve its name only if it replaces the study
of human objects by the study of the various processes
of becoming-an-object. Its role is to found its *knowledge*
on rational and comprehensive *non-knowledge;* that is,
the historical totalization will be possible only if anthropology understands itself instead of ignoring itself. To
understand itself, to understand the other, to exist, to
act, are one and the same movement which founds direct, conceptual knowledge upon indirect, comprehensive knowledge but without ever leaving the concrete—that is, history or, more precisely, the one who
comprehends what he knows. This perpetual dissolution of intellection in comprehension and, conversely,
the perpetual redescent which introduces comprehension into intellection as a dimension of *rational non-
knowledge* at the heart of knowledge is the very ambiguity of a discipline in which the questioner, the question, and the questioned are one.

These considerations enable us to understand why
we can at the same time declare that we are in profound
agreement with Marxist philosophy and yet for the present maintain the autonomy of the existential ideology.
There is no doubt, indeed, that Marxism appears today

to be the only possible anthropology which can be at once historical and structural. It is the only one which at the same time takes man in his totality—that is, in terms of the materiality of his condition. Nobody can propose to it another point of departure, for this would be to offer to it *another man* as the object of its study. It is *inside* the movement of Marxist thought that we discover a flaw of such a sort that despite itself Marxism tends to eliminate the questioner from his investigation and to make of the questioned the object of an absolute Knowledge. The very notions which Marxist research employs to describe our historical society—exploitation, alienation, fetishizing, reification, etc.—are precisely those which most immediately refer to existential structures. The very notion of *praxis* and that of dialectic—inseparably bound together—are contradictory to the intellectualist idea of a knowledge. And to come to the most important point, *labor,* as man's reproduction of his life, can hold no meaning if its fundamental structure is not to pro-ject. In view of this default—which pertains to the historical development and not to the actual principles of the doctrine—existentialism, at the heart of Marxism and taking the same givens, the same Knowledge, as its point of departure, must attempt in its turn—at least as an experiment—the dialectical interpretation of History. It puts nothing in question except a mechanistic determinism which is not exactly Marxist and which has been introduced from the outside into this total philosophy. Existentialism, too, wants to situate man in his class and in the conflicts which oppose him to other classes, starting with the mode and the relations of production. But it can approach this "situation" in terms of *existence*—that is, of comprehension. It makes itself the questioned and the question as questioner; it does not, as Kierkegaard did apropos of Hegel, set the irrational singularity of the individual in opposition to universal Knowledge. But into this very Knowledge and into the universality of concepts, it wants to reintroduce the unsurpassable singularity of the human adventure.

Thus the comprehension of existence is presented as the human foundation of Marxist anthropology. Nevertheless, we must beware here of a confusion heavy with consequences. In fact, in the order of Knowledge, what we know concerning the principle or the foundations of a scientific structure, even when it has come—as is ordinarily the case—later than the empirical determinations, is set forth first; and one deduces from it the determinations of Knowledge in the same way that one constructs a building after having secured its foundations. But this is because the foundation is itself a knowing; and if one can deduce from it certain propositions already guaranteed by experience, this is because one has induced it in terms of them as the most general hypothesis. In contrast, the foundation of Marxism, as a historical, structural anthropology, is man himself inasmuch as human existence and the comprehension of the human are inseparable. Historically Marxist Knowledge produces its foundation at a certain moment of its development, and this foundation is presented in a disguised form. It does not appear as the practical foundations of the theory, but as that which, on principle, pushes forward all theoretical knowing. Thus the singularity of existence is presented in Kierkegaard as that which on principle is kept outside the Hegelian system (that is, outside total Knowledge), as that which can in no way be *thought* but only *lived* in the act of faith. The dialectical procedure to reintegrate existence (which is never *known*) as a foundation at the heart of Knowledge could not be attempted then, since neither of the current attitudes—an idealist Knowledge, a spiritual existence—could lay claim to concrete actualization. These two terms outlined abstractly the future contradiction. And the development of anthropological knowing could not lead then to the synthesis of these formal positions: the movement of ideas—as the movement of society—had first to produce Marxism as the only possible form of a really concrete Knowledge. And as we indicated at the beginning, Marx's own Marxism, while indicating the dialectical opposition between knowing and being, contained implicitly the demand for an existential foundation for the theory. Furthermore, in order for notions like reification and alienation to assume their full meaning, it would have been necessary for the questioner and the questioned to be made one. What must be the nature of human relations in order for these relations to be capable of appearing in certain definite societies as the relations of things to each other? If the reification of human relations is possible, it is because these relations, even if reified, are fundamentally distinct from the relations of things. What kind of practical organism is this which reproduces its life by its work so that its work and ultimately its very reality are alienated; that is, so that they, *as others,* turn back upon him and determine him? But before Marxism, itself a product of the social conflict, could turn to these problems, it had to assume fully its role as a practical philosophy—that is, as a theory clarifying social and political *praxis.* The result is a profound *lack* within contemporary Marxism; the use of the notions mentioned earlier—and many others —refers to a comprehension of human reality which is missing. And this lack is not—as some Marxists declare today—a localized void, a hole in the construction of Knowledge. It is inapprehensible and yet everywhere present; it is a general anemia.

Doubtless this *practical* anemia becomes an anemia in the Marxist man—that is, in us, men of the twentieth century, inasmuch as the unsurpassable framework of Knowledge is Marxism; and inasmuch as this Marxism clarifies our individual and collective *praxis*, it therefore determines us in our existence. About 1949 numerous posters covered the walls in Warsaw: "Tuberculosis slows down production." They were put there as the result of some decision on the part of the government, and this decision originated in a very good intention. But their content shows more clearly than anything else the extent to which man has been eliminated from an anthropology which wants to be pure knowledge. Tuberculosis is an object of a practical Knowledge: the physician learns to know it in order to cure it; the Party determines its importance in Poland by statistics. Other mathematical calculations connecting these with production statistics (quantitative variations in production for each industrial group in proportion to the number of cases of tuberculosis) will suffice to obtain a law of the type $y = f(x)$, in which tuberculosis plays the role of independent variable. But this law, the same one which could be read on the propaganda posters, reveals a new and double alienation by totally eliminating the tubercular man, by refusing to him even the elementary role of *mediator* between the disease and the number of manufactured products. In a socialist society, at a certain moment in its development, the worker is alienated from his production; in the theoretical-practical order, the human foundation of anthropology is submerged in Knowledge.

It is precisely this expulsion of man, his exclusion from Marxist Knowledge, which resulted in the renascence of existentialist thought outside the historical totalization of Knowledge. Human science is frozen in the non-human, and human-reality seeks to understand itself outside of science. But this time the opposition comes from those who directly demand their synthetic transcendence. Marxism will degenerate into a non-human anthropology if it does not reintegrate man into itself as its foundation. But this comprehension, which is nothing other than existence itself, is disclosed at the same time by the historical movement of Marxism, by the concepts which indirectly clarify it (alienation, etc.), and by the new alienations which give birth to the contradictions of socialist society and which reveal to it its abandonment; that is, the incommensurability of existence and practical Knowledge. The movement can *think* itself only in Marxist terms and can *comprehend* itself only as an alienated existence, as a human-reality made into a thing. The moment which will surpass this opposition must reintegrate comprehension into Knowledge as its non-theoretical foundation.

In other words, the foundation of anthropology is man himself, not as the object of practical Knowledge, but as a practical organism producing Knowledge as a moment of its *praxis*. And the reintegration of man as a concrete existence into the core of anthropology, as its constant support, appears necessarily as a stage in the process of philosophy's "becoming-the-world." In this sense the foundation of anthropology cannot precede it (neither historically nor logically). If *existence*, in its free comprehension of itself, preceded the awareness of alienation or of exploitation, it would be necessary to suppose that the free development of the practical

organism historically preceded its present fall and cap-
tivity. (And if this were established, the historical pre-
cedence would scarcely advance us in our comprehension, since the retrospective study of vanished societies
is made today with the enlightenment furnished by
techniques for reconstruction and by means of the
alienations which enchain us.) Or, if one insisted on a
logical priority, it would be necessary to suppose that
the freedom of the project could be recovered in its full
reality *underneath* the alienations of our society and
that one could move dialectically from the concrete existence which understands its freedom to the various al-
terations which distort it in present society. This hypothesis is absurd. To be sure, man can be enslaved
only if he is free. But for the historical man who *knows*
himself and *comprehends* himself, this practical freedom is grasped only as the permanent, concrete condition of his servitude; that is, across that servitude and
by means of it as that which makes it possible, as its
foundation. Thus Marxist Knowledge bears on the
alienated man; but if it doesn't want to make a fetish of
its knowing and to dissolve man in the process of knowing his alienations, then it is not enough to describe the
working of capital or the system of colonization. It is
necessary that the questioner understand how the questioned—that is, himself—*exists his alienation,* how he
surpasses it and is alienated in this very surpassing. It is
necessary that his very thought should at every instant
surpass the intimate contradiction which unites the
comprehension of man-as-agent with the knowing of
man-as-object and that it forge new concepts, new determinations of Knowledge which emerge from the existential comprehension and which regulate the movement of their contents by its dialectical procedure. Yet
this comprehension—as a living movement of the practi-

cal organism—can take place only within a concrete situation, insofar as theoretical Knowledge illuminates and interprets this situation.

Thus the autonomy of existential studies results necessarily from the negative qualities of Marxists (and not from Marxism itself). So long as the doctrine does not recognize its anemia, so long as it founds its Knowledge upon a dogmatic metaphysics (a dialectic of Nature) instead of seeking its support in the comprehension of the living man, so long as it rejects as irrational those ideologies which wish, as Marx did, to separate being from Knowledge and, in anthropology, to found the knowing of man on human existence, existentialism will follow its own path of study. This means that it will attempt to clarify the givens of Marxist Knowledge by indirect knowing (that is, as we have seen, by words which regressively denote existential structures), and to engender within the framework of Marxism a veritable *comprehensive knowing* which will rediscover man in the social world and which will follow him in his *praxis*—or, if you prefer, in the project which throws him toward the social possibles in terms of a defined situation. Existentialism will appear therefore as a fragment of the system, which has fallen outside of Knowledge. From the day that Marxist thought will have taken on the human dimension (that is, the existential project) as the foundation of anthropological Knowledge, existentialism will no longer have any reason for being. Absorbed, surpassed and conserved by the totalizing movement of philosophy, it will cease to be a particular inquiry and will become the foundation of all inquiry. The comments which we have made in the course of the present essay are directed—to the modest limit of our capabilities—toward hastening the moment of that dissolution.

THE WRITINGS of Jean-Paul Sartre have probably been more influential in the West than those of any other thinker and literary figure since the war. M. Sartre's formal impact in the field of psychology and philosophy has come chiefly from his two studies, *Being and Nothingness* and the *Critique of Dialectical Reason,* both of which laid the theoretical foundations for his doctrine of Existentialism. Sartre's concern, however, has been to relate his theory to human response and the practical demands of living. To this end, he has carried his philosophical concepts into his novels and plays, and there subjected them to the test of imagined experience. His uniqueness has been in the success with which he demonstrates the utility of Existentialist doctrine while creating, at the same time, works of the highest literary merit. Thus M. Sartre has become the popularizer of his own philosophical thought.

Jean-Paul Sartre was born in Paris in 1905 and was graduated from the Ecole Normale Supérieure in 1929 with a doctorate in philosophy. He then taught philosophy in Le Havre, Laon, and Paris. While teaching in Paris during World War II, Sartre played a role in the French Resistance. His first play, *The Flies,* was produced in France, despite its message of defiance, during the German occupation. In 1964 Sartre declined the Nobel Prize for Literature.

No Exit and Three Other Plays, The Devil and the Good Lord and Two Other Plays, and *The Condemned of Altona* are available in Vintage Books. Two novels, *The Age of Reason* and *The Reprieve,* and *The Philosophy of Jean-Paul Sartre* (edited by Robert Denoon Comming) are available in the Modern Library.

VINTAGE WORKS OF SCIENCE
AND PSYCHOLOGY